CW00688110

The Knights Templar

An Enthralling History of the Rise and Fall of the Most Influential Catholic Military Order

Free limited time bonus

Stop for a moment. We have a free bonus set up for you. The problem is this: we forget 90% of everything that we read after 7 days. Crazy fact, right? Here's the solution: we've created a printable, 1-page pdf summary for this book that you're reading now. All you have to do to get your free pdf summary is to go to the following website: **https://livetolearn.lpages.co/enthrallinghistory/**

Once you do, it will be intuitive. Enjoy, and thank you!

Contents

Introduction

The Knights Templar is certainly one of the most intriguing organizations that ever existed. It was a military order at first, created to protect the Christian-controlled Holy Land after the First Crusade, but it became much more than a group of devout Christians who wished to fight in the name of God. Throughout a somewhat short but still very powerful period of its existence, the Knights Templar established itself as a dominant military group with distinct customs, traditions, and rules, and it was respected all over Europe. It would receive countless gifts and donations from European rulers and political figures, who would try to honor the holy and graceful deeds of the order. Members of the order would be admired among both commoners, who would almost make them living legends based on the stories they heard, and among the powerful, who would give them command of their armies, grant them strongholds and castles, and make them their advisors. For about two hundred years, the Knights Templar played a big role in the power politics of the known world and continued to stay influential even after its demise.

However, the great popularity and status that the order held in the Christian world would ultimately cause its downfall. At the dawn of the 14th century, after the unsuccessful final attempts of the

Crusaders to regain control of the Holy Land, the Templars would be brought down by the ones who once adored them so much. King Philip IV of France sought to increase his influence and dominate the papacy at the height of the Inquisition's power, and the Templars would be declared criminals. King Philip would start the purge of the Templars, hunting them down and putting them on corrupt ecclesiastical trials, where they would be condemned for being heretics, traitors to the church, and sodomites. By 1314, the Knights Templar had virtually lost all the power that it once held and would soon be destroyed. It is still one of the most fascinating orders, both for the people who admire them and historians who are compelled to find out more about its mysterious nature.

And mystery has surrounded the order since its creation. It always carried this sense of secrecy, of not fully disclosing what was going on behind closed doors, which raised suspicion about the true nature of its deeds. Throughout the years, the Templar Order has been linked to various secret societies, like the Freemasons, with some claiming that the surviving Templars went underground and continued living as the Freemasons. Conspiracies about its connections to different kinds of heresies are also common. According to many, Templars conducted secret, forbidden rituals and gathered powerful artifacts from the Holy Land, which granted them their power. Whether or not these allegations are true (and most of them probably aren't), one thing is for certain—the legacy of the Knights Templar still continues to live on today and manifests in different ways.

This book is for those curious readers who want to know more about the amazing history of the Knights Templar. It is truly a one-of-its-kind topic that continues to excite historians to this day due to the flawed, limited, and common misconceptions and ideas of the order. This book will mainly cover the outstanding two-hundred-year-long history of the Knights Templar. It will dive deep into how the order was created after the First Crusade, how it rose to dominance and stayed in power for all those years, and the causes of its downfall from being the most influential military organization to essentially a myth. In addition, it will also focus on the structure of the order to better explain what kept it so well organized throughout the years. Finally, it will describe some of the figures who played key parts in its history. And, of course, we will talk about the twisted legacy of the Knights Templar.

Part One: Origins of the Order

Chapter 1 – The First Crusade

The First Crusade was a defining moment in world history. Of course, it did not only have immense religious consequences. The First Crusade also completely transformed the political landscape of the known world and disrupted the balance of power that existed prior to it. Ultimately, however, it led to the creation of the Knights Templar; thus, the First Crusade is pivotal in understanding how the order came to exist. This chapter will cover the history of the First Crusade and explain its significance in relation to the formation of the Order of the Templars.

An Unstable Europe

The dawn of the new millennium saw Europe in the midst of all kinds of power struggles and crises. The continent was as divided as ever and was still trying to form its own identity. In Iberia, the *Reconquista* was still underway, with the Catholics trying to reclaim the lost peninsula from the Muslims. The British Isles were unstable due to constant invasions from Scandinavia. The Normans had even found their way into the Mediterranean, having arrived in southern Italy and Sicily, where they established a foothold in these regions as fierce fighters and mercenaries, ready to seek gold and adventure. Germany and France perhaps had the least problems, but even there, constant uprisings plagued the monarchs. In the

East, what was once the great and powerful Eastern Roman Empire was struggling to keep the territories that it had left together, as it was under constant threat from all sides.

Amidst all these major actors was another player in Europe that sought to increase his influence over the continent. That was, of course, the pope. The papacy was constantly trying to remind everyone that it was the highest authority in the Christian world, only second to God himself. It considered itself an institution to which the rulers of all the Christian kingdoms should answer. While the European monarchs were not exactly keen on this idea, there was virtually nothing that they could do about it. The papacy was, in many cases, a thorn in the side of many rulers. Though they all respected the papacy as an institution and recognized its holy nature, this loyalty would prove to be an inconvenience from time to time. The pope would often excommunicate those he believed disobeyed his direct orders or violated the general principles of Christianity.

One of the best examples of this is what happened between Henry IV of Germany and Pope Gregory VII. The pope was a pragmatist who wanted to reform the church and wipe out the corruption that existed within the highest ranks. King Henry, on the other hand, was tired of the papacy's involvement with the internal affairs of Germany. An additional reason behind the escalation of the tension between the two is that Henry controlled most of northern Italy, including Rome, where the papacy was located. Thus, Henry was not content when the pope wanted to centralize Rome's power even more. The disputes eventually led to the excommunication of Henry from the church in 1074 and further instabilities surrounding the power struggles of the papacy.

Henry IV and his supporters were shocked by Pope Gregory's decision to excommunicate the king. Henry's ancestor, Otto I, was crowned by Pope John XII as the emperor in 962 in Rome. Henry had a unique position of power, and he would not give it up easily.

Thus, when the bishops of Germany and northern Italy were summoned to a council at Brixen in 1080, they declared that Pope Gregory had abused the powers given to him by God and proposed that he should be removed from the position. They also nominated the next pope, Wibert, Archbishop of Ravenna, who would eventually be crowned Pope Clement III some four years later in 1084, when Henry IV was finally able to march on Rome and take the city from the papacy's control. He then became the Holy Roman emperor.

Of course, the papacy was not just willing to give up without a fight either. Henry had made it clear that he was ready to take the necessary steps to keep the institution in check. The members that fled the city after its conquest first elected Victor III as the new legitimate pope, one who was independent of Henry or Clement III. But the untimely death of Victor III just a year and a half later made them elect a new pope yet again. This time, it was Cardinal Bishop Odo of Ostia, who would be known as Urban II. However, he still would not be recognized in the lands of the Holy Roman Empire as the legitimate pope, as the German and northern Italian bishops fully supported Clement III.

The Two Popes

Thus, the situation in Europe prior to the start of the First Crusade was pretty messy overall. In a period of uncertainty and instability, the two popes—Clement III and Urban II—coexisted in a weird environment. The former was backed by the most powerful man in Europe at the time, Henry IV. The latter, on the other hand, was elected by the weakened papacy that believed Henry IV had committed a crime against the holiest institution in the world and, therefore, the whole religion.

These differences between the two popes made the Christian world very confused. Clement III was trying his best to reinforce his position as the true pope. He resided in Rome under the protection of Emperor Henry and was very much leading the Catholic Church.

He was acting as the pope should; he contacted different rulers and offered his help, support, and advice. For example, he communicated with the archbishop of Canterbury in England and invited him for a visit to Rome. He also made contact with the Serbs, sending one of their archbishops a traditional pallium—an ecclesiastic vestment worn by the highest-ranking officials of the church. In short, he was acting as the pope should have acted. He had ongoing conversations with different parts of the Christian world and did not interfere too much in internal affairs—something that he had learned was not the wisest thing to do from Pope Gregory.

Urban II, on the other hand, could not even safely enter Rome. He did visit the city on a couple of occasions during the Christmases of 1091 and 1092, but he was forced to stay outside of the walls for most of his visit and departed the city quickly, eager not to overstay his welcome. Plus, he did not have the support of Henry or the bishops of Germany and northern Italy. Urban's efforts to contact the Christian world were more small-scale and, thus, inconsequential. He would occasionally send letters of support and encouragement with his blessings, like in Iberia, where the process of kicking out the Muslims was beginning to be more and more successful. However, Urban could not gain a strong foothold as the legitimate pope, especially when compared to his rival counterpart.

Surprisingly, Urban found a different, rather unusual ally to strengthen his position. That was the Eastern Orthodox Church. An important thing to remember is that the Great Schism saw the division of the Christian Church into the Western Catholic and Eastern Orthodox Churches. The separation, which happened in 1054, was a culmination of the already deteriorating relations between Rome and Constantinople—the two pillars of the Christian world that were still under Christian control. Because of different distinctions that existed between the Latin and Greek cultures and their respective practices of the religion, which were sometimes as petty as whether or not unleavened bread should be used in the sacrament of communion, the Christian Church split in two, forever damaging the relations between the East and the West.

Thus, when Urban II realized that he was not really gaining any considerable progress with Catholic Europe, he turned his attention to the east to try to repair relations with Constantinople as much as possible to have someone back him up. His efforts were met with relative warmth, considering the fact that Urban was effectively the first pope to try and communicate with the Eastern Church after the Great Schism. Both the Byzantine emperor, Alexios I, and the patriarch of Constantinople, Nikephoros III Grammatikos, expressed their sympathies with Urban's wishes to civilly discuss the differences that existed between the two branches. The emperor even invited the pope to Constantinople and proposed that a united council be convened. It would be attended by the senior clergy from both sides to further clarify the distinctions and resolve the existing disputes. The patriarch, on his part, offered his full support to the efforts of reuniting the church, declaring in a private letter to Urban that he desired "with all [his] heart...the unity of the Church."

Urban's move was pretty successful. The relations started to heal and promised a hopeful future with the Western and the Eastern Churches united. Urban now had won the hearts of the Byzantines, even lifting the excommunication of the Byzantine emperor that had been passed in 1081—another sign that their alliance was not something one could just easily look over. Pope Clement could do nothing but watch from the sidelines as his rival slowly achieved a feat that no one had even thought of. When Clement found out about the frequent letters between Urban and Nikephoros, it was too late to act. Urban was victorious in the battle of the two popes, as he repaired the relations with the East and the West and established himself as the leader of the Christian world.

Trouble in the East

While Urban was busy reinforcing his position as the legitimate pope by repairing the relations with the Eastern Church and, therefore, the Byzantine Empire, Emperor Alexios was struggling to keep his vast lands under his control. Once upon a time, the Eastern Roman Empire was the richest, biggest, and most powerful empire in the known world, stretching from the Balkans to the Middle East. It even controlled parts of North Africa. In addition, four out of the five Christian holy sites were under its control. The Byzantines were proud because holding Constantinople, Antioch, Alexandria, and Jerusalem was a pretty big achievement, especially since the West only had Rome, the so-called "Eternal City," which had lost most of its glory after the collapse of the Western Roman Empire.

However, the Byzantine Empire was under constant threat from all sides, which eventually caused its decline. The Byzantines were overextended and could not effectively contain all the invasions. Thus, by 1095, it had lost most of its territories, only being able to hold on to the core regions in eastern Europe, as well as the western parts of Anatolia and some of the lands that bordered the Black Sea. Most importantly, by the 7th century, the empire had lost three of the four holy sites that it once held, with only Constantinople, the capital of the empire, standing strong.

Prophet Muhammad's successors swarmed the Byzantine positions in Asia Minor and the Middle East. While the Byzantines were occupied with defending their territories against invasions from the Bulgars in the north, the Muslims conquered Persia, then Syria, Palestine, and Egypt, seizing Jerusalem, Antioch, and Alexandria in the process. The dominating Umayyad Caliphate managed to conquer all of North Africa and Spain—the lands that were once part of the great Roman Empire and were predominantly occupied by Christians. The Europeans only responded when the threat of the Muslims invading mainland Europe became too close for comfort. After the Muslim forces sacked the city of Bordeaux in 732, the French forces were able to halt their advance at the Battle of Poitiers and drive them back to Iberia. Despite this, the Muslim naval attacks continued in Sicily and parts of southern Italy. The idea of a united Christian effort to stop the Muslims did not exist back then, and it would take some 350 more years for it to develop. Only with the help of the Norman mercenaries were the Christians able to start fighting back in Spain and Sicily.

The Umayyads and their successors—the Abbasids—did treat those they conquered with respect. The rulers permitted the practice of different religions as long as those people paid a special tax. They also did not forbid the pilgrims who wished to visit the Holy Land. However, this would all change with the arrival of the Seljuk Turks. They came from the Eurasian Steppe, and they conquered the caliphate, converting to Islam shortly afterward. The Seljuks were different from the Umayyads and the Abbasids since they were far more vicious when it came to treating people of other religions and cultures. When they seized Jerusalem in 1065, they massacred the Christian population of the city, publicly shaming the patriarch and killing those who opposed them. After that, they proceeded to defeat the Byzantine forces in the decisive Battle of Manzikert in 1071, driving the Christians out of most of Anatolia and conquering the Byzantine city of Nicaea.

Losing Nicaea was disastrous for the Byzantines. Not only was it one of the biggest cities in the empire, but it was also very close to Constantinople, lying some ninety-five kilometers (sixty miles) southwest. There was no doubt that if they weren't stopped, the Turks would continue advancing until they arrived at the capital. Still, Emperor Alexios had not lost all hope. He knew that if Constantinople fell, the Muslims would have another direct gateway to Europe, which, in a way, would have been worse than when they controlled Iberia. At this time, the eastern European nations were not nearly as organized or powerful as the French, who stopped the

Arab threat at Poitiers. Realizing the true scale of the imminent threat, Alexios turned to get aid from the West, sending a desperate letter in early 1095 to Pope Urban, asking for Europe to answer the call to arms.

Deus Vult

Fortunately for Alexios, when the messenger arrived at the Council of Piacenza in March of 1095, Pope Urban had managed to further consolidate his position as the true pope. The biggest development in that regard was the fact that Prince Conrad, heir to Henry IV of Germany, had sworn his loyalty toward Urban and denounced Clement III. Prince Conrad was one of many "defectors" from Henry's (and therefore Clement III's) camp. Many prestigious priests and Henry's own wife had switched sides and declared their support for Pope Urban. So, when Urban called the meeting at Piacenza in German-controlled territory to discuss an array of ecclesiastical issues, it seemed that he had finally grasped the victory in his rivalry with Clement III.

This was the situation with Urban when the Byzantine envoys unexpectedly arrived at Piacenza to deliver the news of the struggling Byzantine Empire and to ask for help from the pope. The whole council was shocked to hear the news. According to the messengers, the Byzantine Empire would not be able to hold off the Turks for long and was in need of immediate help. Urban carefully listened as the envoys delivered the message. He was quick to realize that there was a decision for him to make. He could try to urge the Europeans to go to Alexios's aid and defend against the Turks. This would be a graceful act and would definitely improve his already great relations with the Byzantines. More importantly, however, it was an opportunity for Urban to cement himself as the true leader of the Christian world and unite the church once and for all.

Urban knew that he had a near-impossible task. Assembling Europe's forces was quite a feat to achieve. He did want to help

Alexios, but he needed the armies of different rulers, who would be skeptical of funding an expedition thousands of miles in the east in unknown lands against an unknown foe. This was what was going on in Urban's mind on his way to Clermont, France, in mid-1095. Over the course of the summer, he set out to recruit different powerful Italian and French leaders to his cause. He also sent out envoys to assemble a council of virtually unseen levels of importance at Clermont, which would focus on the ongoing political matters as well as ecclesiastical issues.

When the council assembled in November of 1095, Urban had already managed to sway Raymond of Toulouse, a powerful sponsor, to aid in the campaign. Urban hoped Raymond's help would motivate others to join him. At the council with the clergy and many French knights, whom the pope had also asked to assemble. Urban waited for the end of the council to deliver his speech, in which he described the situation in Anatolia and discussed the importance of Europe's answer to Byzantium's cause. In fact, his description was so terrifying that it almost felt like an over-exaggeration. He urged the Europeans to unite and fight for the same cause. "So let all feuds between you cease, quarrels fall silent, battles end and the conflicts of all disagreements fall to rest. Set out on the road to the Holy Sepulchre and deliver that land from a wicked race!"[1]

The pope's message was so powerful that it was met with a loud response from the assembled. "Deus vult!" the crowd shouted. "God wills it!" The council would be dismissed after this grand finale, still mesmerized by the power of the pope's speech. Urban was pretty content with the outcome too. At Clermont, he did not propose a plan of attack, the route the Europeans should take to the Holy Land, or any other logistical issue for that matter. All those details could wait. He did, however, promise eternal salvation to

---

[1] Somerville, R. (1974).

those who participated and incited his audience, motivating them to follow God's will. After the council, envoys would be sent all over Europe to spread the pope's message. They claimed that those who would answer his call would forever be remembered as heroes.

The March to the Holy Land

Soon enough, the Christian world started answering the pope's call. About thirty thousand people, a pretty sizeable force, were assembled in the end, and they were all motivated by one purpose: cleansing the Holy Land of the Muslim conquerors and reclaiming what had been taken from them. The First Crusade consisted of people of all ages, statuses, and professions, and they all took part for different reasons. A lot of the participants were knights who were there for the glory. They loved adventure and a challenge, and they wanted to make a name for themselves. There were also many commoners, those who had nothing to lose and hoped to get rich or die trying. The others were dedicated Christians. They understood what lay ahead of them and the risks that were involved with journeying to distant lands, but they were willing to sacrifice everything for the sake of their religion and their loyalty to the pope. To all these Crusaders, the First Crusade was like a divine mission, their destiny even, and all of them embraced it in a way that suited them the most.

Still, despite the fact that the assembled force was quite sizeable and deeply motivated to venture to these unknown lands, the problems the Crusaders encountered were difficult to deal with. The most obvious of these problems were the aforementioned logistical issues. For instance, the first wave of the Crusaders, led by French priest Peter the Hermit, consisted mostly of ordinary, poor citizens. They ravaged the German lands and assaulted Jewish communities that lived in the Rhineland region. Of course, those who were massacred and looted had nothing to do with the Crusade, nor did they pose any threat to Peter the Hermit's men. The People's Crusade, as it became known later, was ultimately pretty unsuccessful, and it is not hard to understand why. Upon their entry into Anatolia in October of 1096, they were quickly defeated by the Seljuk forces.

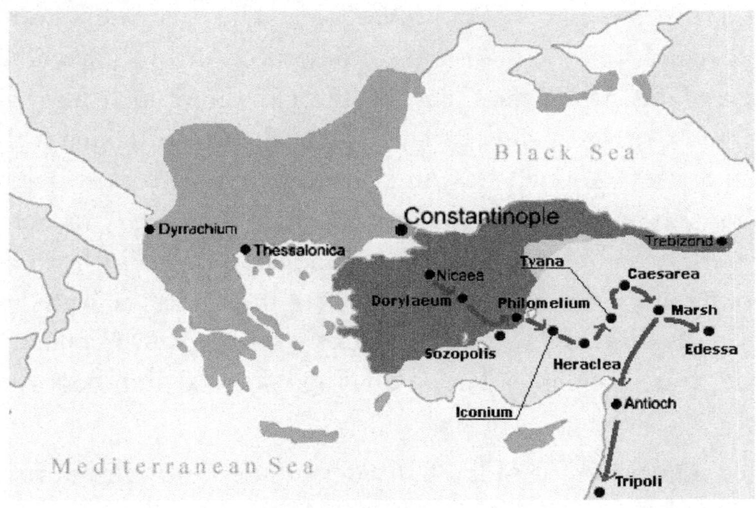

The map of the First Crusade

Gabr-el at English Wikipedia, CC BY-SA 3.0 <https://creativecommons.org/licenses/by-sa/3.0>, via Wikimedia Commons; https://commons.wikimedia.org/wiki/File:Byzantium_after_the_First_crusade.PNG

However, the disastrous People's Crusade would be followed by an effort known as the Princes' Crusade. This time, a more organized force that consisted of trained soldiers and was led by a group of European nobles took on the challenge. Raymond of Toulouse was in charge of the southern French forces, Bohemond of Taranto led a smaller force of Normans from Italy, and Godfrey de Bouillon had assembled the men from Upper and Lower Lorraine. These princes were also joined by several other powerful nobles like Robert Curthose, the son of England's William the Conqueror, and Robert II, Count of Flanders. Together, the army counted almost 100,000 men—a force of unseen size and strength.

The Crusaders saw initial success after they crossed into the Muslim-occupied territory, taking the city of Nicaea with the help of Byzantine ships in June 1097. Then, they successfully defended against an attack at the Battle of Dorylaeum, allowing them to strengthen their position in Anatolia. However, the worst part of their journey was still ahead of them, as the march to the Holy Land was very slow and difficult. The lack of organization and the huge size of the army was disadvantageous. The Crusaders were ill-supplied and suffered thousands of desertions due to starvation and disease. Thus, when they reached the city of Antioch in October 1097, the Crusaders did not fancy their chances of taking it with a frontal assault. Antioch was one of the largest and most defended Muslim cities, so the Crusaders decided to starve it out and prepared the siege in late October. The siege of Antioch would be one of the most tumultuous endeavors of the Crusades, with the city surviving for months while the attackers struggled to maintain high morale and discipline. They continued to lose numbers due to attrition.

The indecisiveness of the Crusaders, paired with misinformation from Stephen de Blois, the son of William the Conqueror who would eventually desert, who claimed that there was no hope of taking the city, caused Emperor Alexios to halt his reinforcements and not come to the aid of the Crusaders. When the Crusaders eventually entered the city in June 1098 after help from the Christian population inside, they decimated the Muslim inhabitants and sacked Antioch to the ground. Just days afterward, they sallied out of the city to defend against the Muslim relief forces and completely routed them. At that point, it became clearer than ever that the Crusaders were ready to move on to their next and final target: the holy city of Jerusalem.

The march to Jerusalem would be even more difficult, with the Crusaders reaching it one year after they had taken Antioch, in June 1099. The Muslims, who were aware of the imminent attack, made the journey to Jerusalem hell for the Christians, evacuating everyone they could from the towns on the way and destroying potential supplies by poisoning the wells and burning down trees. By the time the Crusaders laid siege to the city, they had even fewer means of attacking it than Antioch. They only counted about fifteen thousand men, had little food and water, and not enough supplies to build good siege equipment. Thus, the initial assault in mid-June failed, and the Crusaders were forced to retreat back to their positions. Crucially, in late June, Genoese sailors would arrive at the port of Jaffa, delivering much-needed wood and food to the attackers.

At that point, the Crusaders were fed up with their failed attempts at capturing the city, as well as being ridiculed and taunted by the Muslim defenders, who would often raise crosses on the city walls and mock them. Filled with hatred and further motivated by preachers to take back the city of God, the Crusaders went on to fiercely attack Jerusalem with new siege towers they had constructed with the help of the Genoese. They did not stop their efforts even after they managed to get into the city on July 15th, 1099. The Crusaders were not content with just capturing Jerusalem. They went on to sack it to the best of their ability, massacring all the non-Christians they came across. They showed no mercy to the defeated Muslims. They burned down the mosques, believing that dealing with the Muslims ruthlessly was the only right way of cleansing the Holy City. Overwhelmed with what victory felt like, many of the Crusaders fell on their knees and started praying in the Holy Sepulchre, thanking God for empowering them to fulfill their divine mission. After four very long years, the First Crusade was finally over.

The Aftermath of the First Crusade

The First Crusade was a unique campaign. A united European force had never really been seen before, let alone traveled thousands of miles east to unknown lands, motivated by a holy cause. It is remarkable enough that the effort was made, let alone that it was ultimately successful. In a way, the First Crusade's success was also helped by the relative weakness of their enemy. By the time the Crusaders reached Anatolia, the Muslims were divided and could not set aside their differences to assemble competent enough armies to fight off the invaders. Jerusalem, for example, was held by the Egyptian Fatimids, who were Shi'a Muslims and rivals with the Sunni Turkish Muslims who controlled much of Anatolia. However, the Turkish Muslims were separated into smaller warring kingdoms. Because of this disunity, which was caused by the cultural differences between the Muslim kingdoms, and the inability to produce a united war effort, the Crusaders established four Catholic kingdoms in the conquered lands: the County of Edessa, the Principality of Antioch, the County of Tripoli, and the Kingdom of Jerusalem. Godfrey de Bouillon was the first ruler of the Kingdom of Jerusalem, but he refused to call himself king

instead preferring the title of Protector of the Holy Sepulchre. After his death just one year later, he would be succeeded by his brother, Baldwin I. He would become the first true king of the Kingdom of Jerusalem, and he was crowned at the Church of the Nativity. A Catholic patriarch was also installed in the Holy City, signaling that the newly established territories were independent of any Byzantine influence and were, therefore, European.[2]

The victory obtained in the First Crusade would be celebrated all over the Christian world. People believed that the will of God had been fulfilled. The ones who succeeded and returned home safely would be crowned as legends, while the deserters would forever be damned. Crucially, in the years following the capture of Jerusalem, waves of pilgrims would start venturing out to the Holy Land to experience its divinity firsthand. However, despite the victory of the Crusaders, the route to the Holy Land was still not safe. The pilgrims would be attacked on their way to the holy sites, sparking a need for a force to defend those who wished to visit Jerusalem. What the Latin kingdoms of the East needed was a group of

[2] Frankopan, P. (2012). The First Crusade: The Call from the East. Belknap Press of Harvard University Press. Chapters: 1, 7, 11-12. Napier, G. (2011). The Rise and Fall of the Knights Templar. History Press. Chapter 1.Somerville, R. (1974). The Council of Clermont (1095), and Latin Christian Society." Archivum Historiae Pontificiae, 12, 55-90.

individuals who would devote their lives to the cause of defending all Christians in the Holy Land.

Chapter 2 – Not-so Humble Beginnings

Despite the seemingly impossible challenge, the First Crusade was ultimately successful. The Christians had successfully managed to reclaim the Holy Land and even established European-led kingdoms in the Middle East. It was a proud achievement for all of the Christian world, and it opened up the opportunity for European pilgrims to travel to the lands. However, that task would require much more than sheer will. It would require a force to protect those who wished to pray in the Holy Land. This need led to the creation of the Order of the Templars. This chapter will explore exactly how the Knights Templar originated.

Hugues de Payens

Establishing a foothold in the Holy Land was a pretty significant feat for Europe. After all, it was the fulfillment of God's will; the Christians were destined to return to Jerusalem. Thus, when the news of the triumph reached Europe, there was a wave of pilgrims that wished to travel to the Holy Land. Before the First Crusade, different Muslim rulers would treat the Christian pilgrims differently, with some being more tolerant than others when it came to letting them travel, let alone practice their religion and culture.

But the victory in the First Crusade was an opportunity for the Christians to permanently reclaim what had been lost to the Muslims.

However, there was one problem. More than half of all the Crusaders who managed to survive the campaign had returned home, taking back all the riches they could with them. Those who returned home would be celebrated as heroes and be respected in their communities. Unfortunately for those who wished to stay in the newly conquered Holy Land or travel to it after the Crusade, there was a big issue. There was a shortage of men to defend the Latin kingdoms. The four kingdoms amounted to a small Christian state surrounded by a hostile Muslim world. The Turks, despite their somewhat weakened position, still controlled most of Anatolia, the only path overland that connected the two continents.

Thus, the pilgrims were mistaken when they thought that their "grand return" to the Holy Land would be guaranteed after the victory. Yes, those who wished to take a more expensive sea route from the ports of Venice and Genoa could get to Jerusalem and the other kingdoms relatively safely, but those who wished to travel overland almost always fell prey to the Turks, who were less friendly with the traveling Christians and understandably so. Even those who traveled by sea would encounter all sorts of bandits on their way from the port of Jaffa to the Holy City. These bandits would strip them from all the possessions they had and then oftentimes massacre them.

All in all, there was a need for some kind of a police force to be created to ensure a safer route for the pilgrims. After all, this was the whole reason the Crusade had taken place—to connect the Christians back to their roots. A now-legendary French knight, Hugues (Hugh) de Payens, would take the initiative into his own hands. Not much is known about Hugues de Payens. He was a vassal of the count of Champagne and probably visited Jerusalem while in the count's entourage in 1104. There is speculation that he had been to the Holy Land prior to that visit, but whether or not he actually participated in the First Crusade is not known. He would be the crucial factor in creating the Order of the Templars.

The creation of the order is described as a very noble decision by William of Tyre, a Levantine bishop who wrote about the Templars about sixty years later. According to him, the nine knights, who were led by Hugues de Payens, approached King Baldwin II of Jerusalem in 1118 with a request to grant them the right to protect the "roads and routes against the attacks of robbers and brigands." The nine knights gave away all of their material possessions and devoted themselves to the service of God and the good of all Christians. They would become warrior monks, living together in poverty and vowing to be chaste.[3] These nine knights further developed the concept of the "ideal" or "chivalrous" Christian knight that was so prevalent in the Middle Ages. A lot of European knights had done similar things at the beginning of the First Crusade, such as giving away all of their possessions to the poor to fully dedicate themselves to a greater cause. Hugues de Payens and his companions, in a way, embodied the spirits of those knights, as they sacrificed everything for a noble cause that would not only prove their allegiance to the powerful upper class but also help the poor.

Thus, King Baldwin II of Jerusalem was instantly taken up by the idea of a force of noble individuals that wanted to protect the traveling pilgrims. He granted Hugues de Payens and his men the former Al-Aqsa Mosque as their headquarters. The Al-Aqsa Mosque was one of the biggest and the most sacred mosques in all of the Muslim world, and giving it to the brotherhood whose goal was to directly oppose the Muslims was symbolically significant. There, at the Temple Mount, Hugues de Payens would officially become the leader of the brotherhood. He would be the Master of

---

[3] Napier, G. (2011).

the Temple, and the nine knights would come to be known as the first Templars. The brotherhood would be called the Poor Knights of Christ and the Temple of Solomon, but they are best known as the Knights Templar. Together, they vowed their loyalty to the patriarch of Jerusalem, to live as monks, and fight against those who disturbed the travelers wishing to reach the Holy City.

The First Templars

Besides Hugues de Payens, there is little known about the other founding members of the brotherhood. The most famous was Godfrey de Saint-Omer from Picardy. The others were André de Montbard, Payen de Montdidier, Geoffrey Bisol, Roland, Gondomar, and the final member, whose name we do not know. These nine men were the first Templars. They dwelled in the Al-Aqsa Mosque, living as monks in extreme poverty. It is for this reason that their knighthood is even more impressive, especially when compared to traditional European knights.

The word of the order spread quickly throughout the Christian world. For the first decade of their existence, Templars lived as monks and defended the pilgrims from Jaffa to Jerusalem, just as they had vowed to do. They quickly impressed those who traveled to the Holy Land and even attracted supporters from the West. For example, the Templars came across Fulk V, Count of Anjou, who visited the Holy Land in 1120. The count was very impressed with the noble deeds of the order and offered to show his support by annually gifting them silver. Fulk V was one of the first associates of the Templar Order, with other European nobles following his example.

Thus, by 1127, the Templars had already gained much recognition not only in Outremer (the land of the Crusader States) but also in mainland Europe. This was one of the reasons for their diplomatic mission to France. Organized by Baldwin II, the Templars traveled to Anjou to convince their trusted friend, Fulk V, to marry Baldwin's daughter, Melisende. The count of Anjou was a very powerful noble, which shows the significance of the mission that was entrusted to the Templars. Not only that, but Melisende was also the heiress to the throne of the Kingdom of Jerusalem, meaning that Baldwin was offering Fulk the opportunity to become the next ruler of the kingdom.

In addition to this mission, Grand Master Hugues, who was leading the delegation, had another task to accomplish during his visit to Europe. He needed to recruit more knights to join the order. Baldwin had told Hugues his plans of expanding the Crusader States, and he needed men to fight in what was supposed to be the next Crusade against Damascus. It is not exactly clear whether or not the order had grown or not by this point. While some sources say that there were already around thirty knights in the order, others claim that it still consisted of the original nine. Either way, new recruits would be pretty useful. It would ensure that the order remained strong after the service of the original nine Templars while also providing for a better force to combat the ongoing problem of the endangered traveling pilgrims.

The seal of the Grand Master of the Order of the Knights Templar. Courtesy of Andrew Simsky

https://commons.wikimedia.org/wiki/File:Seal_of_Templars.jpg

It is widely believed that during their visit to Europe, the Templars showed they were not as poor as when they had started out. They had sworn to live in austerity, but the extent to which they went to keep this promise in the early years is truly remarkable. Sources recount the early Templars wearing borrowed, torn clothes since they had given away everything that they owned prior to joining the order. Some speculate that it is why the seal of the Grand Master features two men sharing a horse since it symbolizes their extreme austerity. Despite the fact that the word "poor" would remain in the official name of the order, by the time King Baldwin had sent them on the diplomatic mission to Europe, they had managed to start accumulating some material possessions. They were by no means poor.

The Templar delegation met with many different powerful men of Europe, and each of them was kind enough to donate generous gifts to the order. For instance, Theobald, Count of Blois, and William Clito, Count of Flanders, gifted the order some lands and the right to feudal reliefs on their territories. Others followed the example of Fulk of Anjou and donated gold and silver to Hugues and his companions. Even commoners, who were astonished by the stories of the Templars, which depicted them almost like popular heroes who defended the pilgrims in Outremer, would give them whatever they could, such as clothes and food. A number of people even offered to willingly join the ranks of the Templars, as they were fascinated with the idea of traveling to the city of God and doing the right thing.

All in all, the tour of Europe proved to be pretty successful for the order. By late 1127, they had traveled all over the continent and met the most important figures of the time while also collecting gracious donations and being joined by more men who wished to practice the Templar life. This boosted the popularity of the Knights Templar massively, spreading their name throughout the Christian world and organizing crucial connections that would last for many years to come.

Bernard of Clairvaux and the Council of Troyes

There was one other man who the Templars met that would influence their legacy forever. That man was Bernard of Clairvaux, an abbot who was already known for his charisma and passion for practicing the Christian religion his own way. According to some stories, for example, he jumped in a pool of freezing water when he was a young man to "cool from the heat of carnal longing." After becoming a monk, Bernard joined the famous Cistercian Order at Citeaux with about thirty more of his fellow Burgundian followers. The amazing nature in which he preached, as well as how he led the Cistercians, earned him a name in France. In fact, Hugh of Champagne, after returning home from his second visit to the Holy Land when he came across the Templars, gifted Bernard a piece of his land to establish a new monastery and further expand the Cistercian Order. They renamed the place Clairvaux, Valley of Light, and attracted passionate people from all over France to join them. The Cistercians are also known as the Bernardines, further implying the abbot's significance on the order.

Bernard of Clairvaux

https://commons.wikimedia.org/wiki/File:San_Bernardo,_de_Juan_Correa_de_Vivar_(Museo_del_Prado).jpg

Bernard of Clairvaux and the Cistercian Order firmly believed that true purity could only be achieved by severe austerity and chastity. Thus, he and his followers strictly followed the Rule of Saint Benedict, unlike the majority of the clergy and the ecclesiastic world of the time, which were more associated with luxury. Bernard believed that sacrificing material possessions and struggling was the right way to achieve purity. Therefore, whenever he met the Templars, it was no surprise that he was instantly impressed by them. It is possible that King Baldwin had sent a letter to Bernard prior to Hugues de Payens's visit to Europe, where Hugues asked the abbot to help him devise the official rules of living for the Templars, as well as gain more support in the West. Bernard could have also been aware of the situation in Outremer through Hugh de Champagne since he often contacted the count, who was gracious enough to build the monasteries of the Cistercians and donate to them on many occasions. In addition, André de Montbard, one of the original nine Templars, was Bernard's uncle. Either way, he knew of the troubles in Outremer.

Bernard of Clairvaux would play a crucial role in cementing the Templars' position in Europe and help them finally obtain the recognition that they (or at least King Baldwin) sought in the apostolic world. Thus, on January 13th, 1129, after about a year and a half of the Templar delegation traveling all over Europe and making acquaintances with most of the powerful nobles of the continent, the Council of Troyes would be convened. It would change the fate of the Knights Templar forever. It could be argued that this council was the most significant meeting after the origin of the First Crusade. It was presided by Cardinal Bishop Andrew of Albano, who represented Pope Honorius II. Other influential members of the Christian world were present, such as the archbishops of Sens and Rheims with their own small delegations of bishops. Bernard was also present, despite reportedly suffering from fever, as well as Stephen Harding, who was the new abbot of Citeaux. Theobald of Blois attended the council, and he had very sympathetic views of the Templars and Bernard. Of course, the Templar delegation was also there, with Hugues de Payens as its head.

The Latin Rule of the Templars

Hugues de Payens would be given the honor of giving a speech at the Council of Troyes. In his speech, he would tell of the origins of the Templar Order. At first, he described the grim situation of

Outremer, how the devout pilgrims who wished to visit the Holy City suffered on their way to Jerusalem and how the Latin kingdoms of the East were surrounded by swarms of enemies. He spoke of how the Templars lived, of their austere ways of wearing plain clothes and being allowed only one horse. He also spoke of the Templars sharing everything that they owned. They ate together and tried to avoid any contact with women. Finally, Hugues briefly told them of the hierarchy within the order, saying that the Templars answered to him, the Grand Master, while the order was loyal to the patriarch of Jerusalem.

The council was impressed by Hugues. However, despite the fact that they mostly praised the Templar practices that the Grand Master described, everyone agreed that in order for the Knights Templar to be fully accepted in the Catholic Church as a religious order, they needed a written set of rules that would be ratified by the members of the council. This would ensure the Templars' official "enrollment" as a religious order.

Bernard of Clairvaux would propose drawing up a new official written version of the Templars' way of life. The seventy-three-clause document would become known as the Latin Rule of the Templars. It contained virtually everything about the Knights Templar, from their daily activities to the deeper concepts in which they believed. The Latin Rule of the Templars regulated nearly every aspect of a Templar's life, giving the men a concrete structure they had to follow. With its introduction, the Templar Order would transform its lifestyle to be more Benedictine (following the rule of Saint Benedict). This was due to the influence of Bernard, who himself was a devout Benedictine. Before the Latin Rule, the Knights Templar was considered to have been following the rule of Saint Augustine.

The Latin Rule recognized white as the main color of the Templars' clothing, symbolizing the fact that the Templars had put the darkness of their life behind them. The white habit became synonymous with the Templars, even though the iconic red cross was not added until later. White should have only been worn by the actual members of the order, while their sergeants and squires were required to wear either black or brown clothing. Only those who were deemed "Knights of Christ" were worthy of wearing white, at least according to the Latin Rule. In addition to this, everything the Templars wore needed to be easy to put on and take off; for example, it should not have any additional laces. This detail further underlined the simplicity of their life.

Knights Templar in their typical attire
https://commons.wikimedia.org/wiki/File:Knights-templar.jpg

The Latin Rule also regulated how the order should treat newcomers, saying that boys should not be accepted until they were able to wield weapons and bear arms. It also underlined that brothers should only serve until the end of their fixed term and be allowed to return to secular life afterward. There were rules about the misconduct of the Templars and how they should be dealt with. Generally, the Latin Rule was pretty strict. It treated nearly all misdemeanors, from deserting the battlefield to leaving the castle without permission, with the same severity: expulsion. A lot has been said about the discipline and the strict hierarchy within the order. The Grand Master was the true, supreme leader of the Templars. He oversaw every possible thing that was concerned with the order. He had virtually unrestricted power, and every Templar would have respected him. Not only that but his word was almost thought to have been as important as the word of God himself, showing the allegiance that the Templars had toward their leader.

The physical appearance of the Templars was also noted. Beards and monks' tonsures were mandatory to further promote the sense of equality and brotherhood in the order. The Latin Rule proposed two meals a day that should be silent and communal—one at noon and the other at dusk—with meat only being allowed three times a week. Of course, any physical relationships with women were prohibited. The Latin Rule also underlined that Templars should be occupied with something at all times; chatting and just relaxing during their free time was forbidden. Instead, they should pray, organize clothing and equipment, or work in the stables. The number of horses for each Templar was also increased to three.

The Latin Rule organized the daily routine of the Knights Templar. It pointed out what the brethren should do at different hours of the day. The routine was pretty similar to the normal routine of a regular Catholic monk. This detail is important to understand in a wider context. Since most of the members of the council who drew up the Latin Rule were members of the clergy, the Latin Rule focused heavily on the matters that they were more aware of, which means they did not include much about the military aspects of the order. The Knights Templar was not, after all, a traditional religious order. The whole reason behind its creation was to deal with military matters. Templars were as much knights as they were monks. This was a unique combination that had never been seen before; thus, it was not understood very well.

Over time, new rules would be added, and the document would be expanded to include up to seven hundred clauses in total by the end of the 13th century. These new rules would contain more details about the different aspects of a Templar's life, including more emphasis on the military side of things. It would also be translated into French to be more accessible to the Templars. This was also an unprecedented development, taking into consideration the "superiority" of the Latin language over the other European languages in the Middle Ages, especially in ecclesiastical matters.

Transforming the Concept of Knighthood

All in all, the Templars' visit to Europe turned out to be more successful than they could have imagined. They managed to gain the international recognition that they so desperately needed, with many of the most powerful men in Europe fully supporting their existence. In addition, thanks to Bernard of Clairvaux and the Council of Troyes, they were officially accepted into the Catholic Church and had the backing of important members of the faith. Not only that, but they had also grown their ranks, returning home with men who wished to journey to Outremer and serve in the order. King Baldwin had also accomplished his goal of swaying the count of Anjou, and it was almost certain that he would get the help that he needed from the West to help him fight off the Muslims in the Holy Land.

Spreading the word about the incorporation of the Knights Templar into the Catholic Church meant that there would be, without a doubt, some criticisms aimed toward the order. The most famous one was a letter signed by Hugo Peccator or Hugh the Sinner. While the exact author of this letter is not known, it is thought to be the work of theologian Hugh of Saint Victor. The author seemed to be skeptical about the nature of the order, calling the members people with "no wisdom." He criticized the role of the warrior monk and the implications that might come with it. Hugh warned the Templars not to be tempted by the Devil since he had the power to twist their will and corrupt them. He wanted the Templars to constantly be working on themselves, to try to understand their inner state and strive for personal salvation. For him, killing and hating one's enemies were devilish temptations, and he was worried the Templars might not be able to protect themselves from letting the Devil enter their hearts.

Similar criticisms came from other religious personas. Prior Guigo of the Carthusian Order, for example, also sent a letter to Hugues de Payens sometime in 1129, reminding the Grand Master not to mix the military side of the Knights Templar with the religious side. He stressed that in order for the Templars' killings to be justified, they should first "purge [their] souls of vices, then the lands from the barbarians."

These criticisms were defended by none other than Bernard of Clairvaux in his work called *In Praise of the New Knighthood* (*De laude novae militia*). In fact, he had been asked by Hugues de Payens to write such a document in light of the criticisms. It was originally written in Latin sometime after the Council of Troyes, presumably in the first part of the 1130s. The document strongly supported the idea of the warrior monk and praised the deeds of the Knights Templar. Bernard called the Templars and Hugues the "knights of Christ" and "Grand Master of the knights of Christ," respectively. He recognized the Templars as being a new separate form of knighthood, at least in comparison with the old concept that had originated in Europe after the collapse of the Roman Empire. He claimed that the Templars were the embodiment of the new ideal of knighthood, combining the monastic with the military and fighting in the name of God.

Traditionally, knights would serve their masters and get payment in return, which they would spend to either purchase lands and rise up in the ranks or get better, flashier equipment. Many knights who ventured to the Holy Land during the First Crusade searched for glory and praise, and they were hoping that reclaiming Jerusalem would bring them that. While they were certainly not wrong, Bernard claimed that the purpose of the Templars stood higher than all of them. There was nothing wrong with killing in the name of Christ. He distinguished between the "regular" form of killing, which would be murder, and the killing of evil. The former was undoubtedly a sin, while the latter was not. It was justified. Bernard even went as far as to say that not only those who would die for Christ could attain salvation but also those who killed in his name. In other words, he tried to prove that the Knights Templar was not only an honorable organization due to its exceptional monastic lifestyle but also because of its military side.

This distinction of the Templars representing a new higher form of knighthood played a vital role in the order's developing stages. In some sense, the Templars fully embraced the status that Bernard of Clairvaux had granted them. After all, the differences between the old and the new knights were apparent. The purpose of the old knight can clearly be seen even from his appearance: colorfully painted shields and lances, silk cloths and expensive armor for their horses, excessive attention to detail, and expensive gold or silver-plated ornaments all over their equipment. This appearance expressed their prior success, wealth, and status as knights. The flashy appearance of a traditional knight can be considered a sign of his innate motives, which, more often than not, had nothing to do with serving God. Bernard even compared knights to women due to their focus on appearances.

Templars were, in a way, the next step in the evolution of the image of the knight. They did not exist to fight for those who paid them the most or to rise up in the ranks or buy better equipment as a sort of upgrade. They did not perform actions for praise. Instead, they were warriors of God. They were the representation of what a Christian knight should be. The idea that had been mentioned by

Pope Urban II at the Council of Clermont was further underlined and supported by Bernard. The pope had remarked that war against evil was just, while Bernard claimed that the true warriors of justice were the Knights Templar, as they fought against the looming evil in Outremer.

The pope was right to assume that the Crusading knights would be motivated to fight for a noble, pious cause. And while a good portion of the Crusading knights did genuinely go to war to reclaim the Holy Land, it was apparent that their initial motivations were overshadowed by their lust and greed, whereas the Templars had no such feelings since they lived the life of a monk. The introduction of the Knights Templar was followed by a subtle paradigm shift that affected both the church and the aristocracy of Europe. Templars were respected because of their devotion to their distinct, never-before-seen warrior monk lifestyle. After their appearance on the international scene, other knights were also expected to live by the Christian code of ethics as well.

Thus, those who were critical of the Templar Order's purpose and structure, although relatively few in number, were met with quite a fierce defense from one of the biggest allies of the Templars. With *In the Praise of the New Knighthood*, Bernard of Clairvaux further justified the creation of the Knights Templar. Instead of perceiving the "job" of a warrior monk as being nearly impossible to successfully pursue, he saw it as a noble cause that was only meant for the strongest in mind and body. His differentiation of "homicide" (sinful killing) and "malecide" (the killing of evil) was also crucial. It meant that the deeds of the Templars were not up to interpretation; they should not be judged by others because of their purpose. After all, the Templars had received blessings from King Baldwin, who granted them one of the most important holy sites in Jerusalem, as well as from the patriarch of Jerusalem. And now, they were backed by the majority of the Catholic Church in the West.

The trip to Europe was a stunning success. As the Templar delegation sailed back to Outremer, having established strong connections with the most powerful men of the West, the future of the order looked promising—and it certainly would be.[4]

---

[4] Napier, G. (2011). *The Rise and Fall of the Knights Templar.* History Press. Chapter 2.

Hill, P. (2018). *The Knights Templar at War, 1120-1312.* Pen & Sword Military. Chapter 1.

Barber, M. C. (1984). "The Social Context of the Templars." *Transactions of the Royal Historical Society,* 34, 27-46.

Martin, S. (2011). *The Knights Templar.* Oldcastle Books.

Chapter 3 – The Return to Outremer

This chapter looks to explore the period after the Templars' visit to Europe up to the Second Crusade. By that time, the Knights Templar had managed to become pretty successful. It was now officially recognized in the West and was supported by the Christian world. The years that followed would only see the power of the Templars increase almost exponentially. They would become more and more involved in the important affairs of Outremer.

Damascus

The Templar delegation returned to Outremer in May 1129. Count Fulk of Anjou was also with them, having agreed to marry Melisende, King Baldwin's heiress. The king was fascinated by the success of the European tour. The Templars had achieved everything that he had desired. Through the recognition of the Templars, Baldwin also managed to raise the West's awareness of the situation in the Holy Land. He desperately needed men to fight for him, but the fight was not necessarily going to be defensive. Yes, attacks on Christian lands were still happening, but Baldwin had different goals in mind. He had his eyes fixed on Damascus.

Not only was the ancient city of Damascus one of the richest in the Near East, but it was also strategically very important. It was located about fifty miles from the Mediterranean, making it too close for comfort to the narrow stretch of Crusader-controlled lands. With enough effort and coordination, whoever ruled Damascus could control the land supply chains between the northern and southern parts of the Crusader States. The Muslim world was still not unified back then, and King Baldwin looked closely for a potential opportunity to take the city, as it would be a good outpost against future threats that came from Syria. Crucially, Tughtigin, the atabeg of Damascus, had passed away a year before the Templars' return to Outremer. The city was under the control of his son, Buri, who was not nearly as proficient at ruling as his father.

Buri had bad relations with a very important organization in Damascus: the Assassins. The Order of the Assassins was a secular sect of Shi'a Islam, and its aim was the elimination of powerful individuals who were considered potential threats. The problem was that Damascus was predominantly a Sunni Muslim city; thus, the Assassins were often frowned upon by the population. Atabeg Tughtigin had dealt with this issue by granting the Assassins control of the fortress of Banias, from which they conducted their operations. Buri, perhaps succumbing to the pressure due to being a young and inexperienced leader, started a purge of the Assassins in the autumn of 1129, causing unrest and riots throughout the province. The leader of the Assassins, Ismail, approached King Baldwin for help and offered him the fortress of Banias for protection.

Baldwin, of course, could not let this perfect opportunity get away. He called for help from the rest of the Latin kingdoms of the East and assembled an army with the count of Tripoli, the count of Edessa, and the prince of Antioch in late 1129. A squadron of Templars, including those recruited from Europe by Hugues de

Payens, was also in the army. King Baldwin marched to Banias in November, where he came across the forces from Damascus. Atabeg Buri had stationed his army between Baldwin and the fortress and was waiting for the Crusaders to come to him. Baldwin, however, was hesitant to advance and stalled the stand-off.

The action started when a small force led by William of Bures decided to start pillaging the settlements near the fortress. They were ambushed by the Damascene vanguard about twenty miles from the main Crusader camp. The Damascene cavalrymen, who knew the landscape, destroyed the breakaway force, with only forty-five men surviving. Baldwin decided to advance quickly on the enemy forces after he heard the news of the ambush from the survivors. Unfortunately for him, heavy rain made it impossible for his army to go farther, and the attackers were forced to retreat.

This assault was King Baldwin's second failed attempt to capture Damascus. He had only managed to raid the surroundings of the city in 1126, and he was now forced to go back. Also, after crossing back to the Christian-controlled lands, the reinforcements that he had from the other Latin kingdoms also returned to their homes. This meant that Baldwin's chances of snatching Damascus had faded, as assembling a competent enough force would be more difficult as time passed. All in all, the failure to capture Damascus would prove to be fatal for the Crusaders in the long run.

The Three Papal Bulls

The failure to take Damascus did not really affect the Knights Templar. In a way, it further cemented their status as warriors against the forces of evil. We should not forget that the original goal of the Templars was to protect the pilgrims on their way to Jerusalem from the swarms of bandits that ambushed them. However, their transition from that role to fighters for the king of Jerusalem seemed very natural. It is as though it was a given from the very beginning. Although their exact identity is unknown, the

Templars who participated in the Damascus campaign were skilled warriors.

The Damascenes had technically nothing to do with the pilgrims traveling to Outremer. Thus, the Templars technically should have had nothing to do with the Damascenes. But they did go to fight against them, signaling that their duties were not limited to dealing with bandits and thieves. Plus, it was still a noble cause. It can be argued that the Templars joined Baldwin's forces because they already considered the Muslims at Damascus as a threat, and the fact they fought against them made the Damascenes a legitimate "evil." Therefore, the actions of the Templars were justified back then, even if Baldwin's motivations included capturing the rich city just to expand his power in Outremer, not for defensive purposes.

After Damascus, the Templars' wealth started growing exponentially, thanks to the gracious donations the order received from all over the world. Gifting money, lands, castles, and different resources became a pretty common way for the givers to prove their piety. In fact, it was considered just as pious of a deed as contributing to building churches and directly supporting the clergy. The Templars themselves, of course, never really asked for donations since they followed the Benedictine lifestyle as outlined in the Latin Rule.

Among these avid supporters of the order was Pope Innocent II. Despite the fact that, in the 1130s, he still was not the one true, legitimate pope (he did not even dwell in Rome, unlike his rival, Pope Anacletus II), Innocent made sure that he showed his gratitude. After the Council of Pisa, which he had called in 1135, Pope Innocent collected a mark of gold and silver from the clergy each year and sent it to Outremer.

Pope Innocent's support would become even clearer with the issue of the first of three papal bulls that were concerned with the Knights Templar. In 1138, his rival, Anacletus, died. Innocent's supremacy was not to be challenged. A year later, he issued the first bull, named *Omne datum optimum,* a document that gave a list of privileges to the order. It was the first official, written evidence of papal support for the Templars. The first bull underlined the fact that the Templars were fighting in the name of Christ and were the defenders of the Christian faith. It also made it clear that the Grand Master of the Templar Order was to be elected by the brothers themselves without any outside interference, and it expanded his duties and rights as the head of the order.

This may have been the result of the influence of the newly elected Templar Grand Master, Robert de Craon, who succeeded Hugues de Payens after his passing in 1136. Robert de Craon was not only a great warrior. He was also known for his organizational skills. After his election, the new Grand Master would make it his goal to find official support for the order with help from the papacy. It could be argued that the first papal bull was a fruitful result of his efforts.

Alongside these points, the bull exempted the Templar Order from paying tithes and promised the order it could keep all spoils that were retrieved from the Muslims during their fighting. In addition, the bull granted the order the right to build chapels and churches and recruit members of the clergy to come and reside there. The leaders of the order were able to offer the clergy to stay as permanent members of the brotherhood after one year of serving, but they also had the right to expel them as they saw fit. In short, the papal bull gave the Templars an amazing opportunity to further grow their order, and it underlined how the order could boost its income and ensure stability.

The privileges of the Knights Templar would increase in the following years, as the new popes would introduce two more papal bulls. After *Omne datum optimum*, Pope Celestine II would issue *Milites Templi* in 1144, urging the clergy to collect resources for the Templars in exchange for one-seventh of their penance's remittal. Furthermore, it gave the Templars further access to the Christian churches of the world and made sure that they were received and treated with respect and care. *Militia Dei*, which was issued by Pope Eugenius III a year later, further consolidated the Templars' position. It gave them the right to collect their own tithes from the properties they owned, as well as bury their dead in their churches unless they had been excommunicated.

The three papal bulls put the Knights Templar at the center of the Christian world. It legitimized the order and gave them unseen levels of respect and privilege. By 1145, the Order of the Templars stood higher than virtually any other similar organization. It even had the firm backing of the papacy. Though there were some criticisms about granting the Templars this much independence and exclusive rights, there was nothing the critics could do to reverse the changes that had already been made and legitimized by the bulls. Due to the popes' efforts to show their support, the order would keep growing in size and wealth from other sources. The Templars participated in numerous military campaigns in Outremer for the good of Christianity, and they were generously rewarded for their noble efforts. The three bulls were issued to build on the previous successes of the order, with donations and funding swarming in.

The Templars in Iberia

The Templars would gain a strong foothold in the Iberian Peninsula, which began in the early years of their existence. Iberia was dominated by the Moors (which was a term Christians used to call Muslims, primarily those who were in Iberia or North Africa). They controlled the southern part of the peninsula by the 12th century. The Christians, however, had already started a (somewhat) united offensive to drive the Muslims out of the lands, which they considered to be Christian. The *Reconquista* was one of the most significant yet drawn-out and disoriented war efforts in history, and it lasted for centuries. Over time, progress was made by the Christian kingdoms to reconquer the lost lands. By 1085, King

Alfonso VI of Castile had captured the central city of Toledo, weakening the Muslims' position.

Alongside the Kingdom of Castile and León—an entity that would change from time to time to include the names of both or just one of the two provinces until it finally united in the 13th century—there was the Kingdom of Aragon and the smaller but just as fierce counties of Barcelona and Portugal (which became a kingdom in 1139). These states fought to drive the Muslims out of the peninsula, but oftentimes, they had internal problems and even challenged each other for supremacy in the region. The fight for Iberia became very important, almost like another Crusade, with Pope Paschal II even declaring that the sins of those who fought for the reinstitution of Christianity in Iberia would be remitted, just like in the First Crusade.

The Iberian kingdoms had already organized military orders or rather confraternities of knights to combat the Muslim threat at the beginning of the 12th century. After the rapid expansion of retrieving lands, Alfonso I of Aragon founded the Confraternity of Belchite in 1122 and the Order of Monreal in 1124. These confraternities were similar to the Knights Templar in the sense that their purpose was to combat the existing Muslim threat. The main difference is that they were not composed of warrior monks, and the knights who wished to join them did not have to live monastic lives. They were not Christian orders. Rather, they were communities of Christian knights that were employed by King Alfonso to fight the Moors in the south. Similar to the Templars, they were given different fortresses and small towns to conduct their operations from, and while they saw initial success, both confraternities would soon meet their end, as they could not deal with the overwhelming Muslim forces. Still, the main purpose of the confraternities was to provide military support to the king's forces and to patrol strategic lands, like narrow passes and valleys.

The appearance of the Templars in Iberia would prove to be a pivotal point for the *Reconquista.* It is logical to assume that the Templars first entered the peninsula during their visit to Europe when they had traveled all over the continent to spread the word about the formation of their order and gather any type of support they could. Interestingly, they first became involved in Portugal rather than in other Spanish kingdoms. At the time of their arrival, sometime in 1128, Portugal was not in the best of situations. There was a political crisis going on between Queen Teresa and her son, Afonso Henriques. Young Afonso had gathered support from Galician nobles, and he wanted independence from his mother. After a period of struggle and the important Battle of São Mamede, this would be granted to him in June of the same year. A couple of months before that, in March, Queen (technically Countess) Teresa would grant the Templars their first documented holding in Iberia: the Castle of Soure, which was located about fifty miles south of the town of Coimbra. Prince Afonso would regift the castle to the Templars after he seized power from his mother. While this action may seem a bit unnecessary, by doing so, Afonso could confirm his support to the Templars.

Gifting the Castle of Soure to the Templars was not, of course, only a matter of showing gratitude for their deeds in Outremer or simply a pious act by young Afonso. It also hinted that he wanted the order to stay in his lands and grow and possibly even help him in future wars against the Muslims. The Templars, however, at that point in time, simply did not have enough members to properly run the castle, let alone reinforce Afonso's army with their elite skills.

Still, Iberia was in an all-out war. The Christian kings in the peninsula did not have enough resources to spare some for the Templars, who would just take them back to Outremer. Although gathering support and donations to take back to the Holy Land was the initial intent of the Templars, the ongoing situation in Iberia would have made them stay and take part in the *Reconquista.* Plus,

Soure was a castle of strategic importance, located right on the front lines, further encouraging the order to set up, search and recruit more brothers, and actively defend their position. In addition, the confirmation of the fact that Soure was Templar property, paired with Afonso's declaration of brotherhood to the order, meant that he would have more reasons for the legitimization of his rule. After all, he had rebelled against his mother and made himself the ruler. All in all, it would create a good image for the young prince, as well as encourage the Templars to fight with him or for him in upcoming battles.

The remains of Castle

The Templars' presence in Portugal would only increase after that. There are documents that confirm more lands were granted to them in the region. However, the Templars would not actively get involved in battle before 1144. The main explanation for this is that the expansionist Afonso was mainly concentrated on pushing his borders against other Christian states. Thus, the Templars would not agree to fight with him against other Christians, as it would go against their code. It is logical to think that they only grew their numbers and power from 1128 until they finally joined the *Reconquista* in 1144 after the Moors attacked their castle at Soure. Unfortunately, they were defeated, as the Muslims heavily outnumbered the brothers, who did not get much help from King Afonso.

But this did not stop the Knights Templar from continuing to spread their influence in Portugal; it just means that the Templars were not directly involved in major campaigns in the *Reconquista* until 1147. At this time, King Afonso fully consolidated his power at home and started going on the offensive against the Moors. The Templars would assist the king at the Battle of Santarém in March 1147 and then, with the combined forces of the Second Crusade, join him in capturing Lisbon. This would further boost their position in Iberia. King Afonso granted them the churches of Santarém, and later on, they would gain control of the Castle of Cera. All in all, the Templars would gain a significant foothold in Portugal, and over the years, they increased their presence as they fought for Christian Portugal against the Muslim threat.

In Spain, the Templars appear to have gained their first bit of land in 1130, two years later after they did so in Portugal. Raymond Berenguer III, Count of Barcelona, granted the order the Castle of Granyena in July and also joined them as an associate member. His son, Raymond Berenguer IV, would continue what his father had started and form a pretty warm relationship with the Templars over the years in Barcelona—something that would prove to be vital in the years to come.

An extraordinary development for the Knights Templar occurred when King Alfonso I of Aragon had the order mentioned in his will. King Alfonso, fittingly nicknamed "The Battler," had expanded the lands of Aragon significantly during his rule and weakened the power of the Muslims in the region. We should also not forget his love for the military orders, which he would establish to help him defend the newly conquered lands from those who wished to take them back. Unfortunately, Alfonso of Aragon had no heirs, and when he died in 1134, securing the whole of his kingdom proved to be a problem. Knowing that various Spanish nobles would seek to take over parts of his lands and wanting to avoid the dissolution of the kingdom that he had created, Alfonso declared in his will that he left the Kingdom of Aragon and Navarre to "the Orders of the Temple, St. John of Jerusalem and the Holy Sepulcher."[5]

This move was certainly ambitious and, in some sense, reckless, and it certainly confused his kingdom. A military order could not rule a whole kingdom. Alfonso's younger brother, a monk named Ramiro, would save the Kingdom of Aragon and Navarre from collapse. Ramiro realized that someone needed to act for the future of the kingdom, so he came out of the monastery and raised a child that would later be betrothed to Raymond Berenguer IV, who was already the count of Barcelona at the time. With this move, Raymond Berenguer managed to become a legitimate king of Aragon in 1150.

Raymond Berenguer would play an important part in resolving the matter of Alfonso's will. The late king had left the whole kingdom to the Christian orders of the East, not only the Templars but also the Knights Hospitaller (although the latter was not nearly as present in Iberia as the former). Raymond knew that he could not just ignore these orders, believing that would be an unjust act. However, he also recognized that he would need them in the fight for the peninsula. This was where his tight relations with the Knights Templar came in. Because of his family's history with the order, Raymond was able to come to an agreement with the Templars in November of 1143. Grand Master Robert of Craon attended the ceremony in Girona, where the Templar Order would receive six

[5] Lourie, E. (1975).

important castles in Aragonese lands, along with the territories that surrounded them.

This was, by far, the biggest amount of land the order had received by that point. The six castles of Monzon, Mongay, Barbara, Chalamera, Belchite, and Remolins were, in a way, an investment from Raymond. He needed the Templars to stay and reinforce his armies, and with this act, he established a sense of trust and permanent connection between the order and the throne. Along with the lands, he promised the order a tithe of all royal revenue, a fifth of all lands conquered from the Muslims, and several other yearly payments and economic benefits, like exemption from taxes and customs. He hoped all of this would motivate the Templars to build up their possessions in Iberia and fight in the *Reconquista*.

The Templars became a force to be reckoned with in the Iberian Peninsula, even though they were thousands of miles away from their home base in Jerusalem. Unlike the rest of Europe, the Iberian lords actually needed the help of the Templars; other European nobles gave them donations for their goodwill and piety. After all, the Iberians were in a war against the Muslims to take back what was once theirs, and the order fit their requirements perfectly. The castles the Templars received in the peninsula were of strategic importance and almost forced the Templars to the front lines.

And the Templars certainly delivered. They aided the Iberian lords numerous times during the *Reconquista*, further boosting their popularity. With their success came more lands, more privileges, and more respect, so much so that it can be argued that by the time of their downfall in the late 13th century, the Templars were significantly present in Iberia. We shall return to the order's ever-increasing role in the peninsula later on, but before that, it is important not to forget about contemporary developments in

Outremer, where the Templars would be needed against an emerging threat.[6]

[6] Valente, J. (1998). "The New Frontier: The Role of the Knights Templar in the Establishment of Portugal as an Independent Kingdom." *Mediterranean Studies*, 7, 49-65. http://www.jstor.org/stable/41166860.

Lourie, E. (1975). "The Will of Alfonso I, 'El Batallador,' King of Aragon and Navarre: A Reassessment." *Speculum*, 50(4), 635-651. https://doi.org/10.2307/2855471.

Hill, P. (2018). *The Knights Templar at War, 1120-1312*. Pen & Sword Military. Chapter 3.

Martin, S. (2011). *The Knights Templar*. Oldcastle Books. Chapter 1.

Chapter 4 – The Second Crusade

We have now looked at the early period of the Templars' existence. Due to the exceptional premise of the organization, which included the merging of two different lifestyles of the monk and the knight, the Templars managed to gain a significant following pretty early on. They earned their name in the Christian world with the help of powerful Europeans and members of the church, which boosted their popularity higher and higher, eventually making them the most well-known Christian order. In this chapter, we shall take a look at a historical development that can be considered the final step to the Knights Templar finally cementing their position as the most important military organization. The Templars played a pretty big role throughout the course of the Second Crusade. All in all, their involvement would take them to highs that nobody could have expected.

The New Possessions

Robert de Craon, the new Grand Master of the Templars, was a much more administratively-minded leader than his predecessor, Hugues de Payens. Robert had taken the position in 1136, and since his election, the Templars' power seemed to increase exponentially. Under Robert de Craon's leadership, the Templars realized the potential their order had. We have already discussed their gains in Iberia, where the Templars would grow stronger and stronger. A partial reason for this was the need for experienced fighters against the Muslims during the *Reconquista*, and it was a role that was perfect for the Templar Order. The Templars became a valuable asset for Iberian lords against the Moors, and over time, they would be granted more and more possessions.

Robert de Craon was directly involved in much of the process of forming relations with the Iberian kingdoms from the very beginning. He was present at Girona when King Alfonso's will was discussed. So, we can assume that he believed the order could benefit in a similar way in the Holy Land as it did in Iberia. In the mid-1130s, the Templars received more castles in Outremer, the first of which were situated north of their center of operations in Jerusalem in the Principality of Antioch.

Sometime around 1136 to 1137, the order received its first holdings in the Amanus Mountains, some sixteen miles from the city of Antioch. It was a strategically important location. The place was known as the Belen Pass, and it connected Antioch with Cilician Armenia. The Templars were assigned to guard the pass, which

Ruins of Baghras, viewed from the west side

No machine-readable author provided. Godfried Warreyn assumed (based on copyright claims)., CC BY-SA 3.0 <http://creativecommons.org/licenses/by-sa/3.0/>, via Wikimedia Commons https://commons.wikimedia.org/w/index.php?curid=627601

was originally used by the First Crusaders to cross from Armenia into the Holy Land. The fortress of Gaston, originally known as Baghras, which the Templars received, was one of the gateways to Syria. Along with Gaston, the Order would also gain possession of La Roche-Guillaume and La Roche de Roussel, which were both important fortresses built in mountainous regions to patrol the passes to the Latin kingdoms. The Templars would also be granted the castle at Darbask and the Port of Bonnel on the Gulf of Ayas later on.

The order would also see some love from the new king of Jerusalem, Fulk, who succeeded Baldwin in 1131. In his efforts to consolidate his position in the south against the Fatimid Caliphate of Egypt, he made sure to mobilize the military orders in his possession and entrust them with the running of strategically important points. The Templars already held the Castle of Latrun, which they used to patrol the way from Jaffa to Jerusalem. It was an important road that was used by the pilgrims to travel to the Holy

Land. In 1139, King Fulk also gave them the castle in Gaza. In short, their presence would increase in Outremer, as the lords of the Latin kingdoms realized their potential in defending the Holy Land against the Muslims.

Since their creation, the Crusader States were almost fully (with the exception of Cilician Armenia) surrounded by Muslim lands that were hostile to them. Fortunately for the Christians, for some time, the Muslims were divided amongst themselves and did not pose as big of a threat to the newly established Christian kingdoms. However, as the Crusader States observed their enemies mobilize, they started counting more on whatever help they could get, and the Knights Templar was one of the best solutions to their problems.

A New Threat

The Latin kingdoms would not face much resistance directly after their formation at the end of the First Crusade. Again, this was caused by the disunity of the Muslims in Anatolia and the Middle East and their inability to find some kind of an agreement between the Shi'as and the Sunnis. Baldwin's campaigns against the Damascenes were, as we already remarked, more of a wish to expand rather than an answer to direct aggression.

The situation would change in the late 1130s, however, as much of the Muslim world would start to unite under one leader. His name was Imal al-Din Zengi, the Atabeg of Mosul. In 1128, he managed to capture the city of Aleppo, challenging the supremacy of the Damascenes in Syria. In fact, just like King Baldwin of Jerusalem, he wanted to take Damascus for himself to consolidate his power in the region and emerge as the leader of the Sunni Muslims. King Fulk and the other leaders of the Latin kingdoms in Outremer observed Zengi carefully, eventually recognizing him as the biggest threat to the integrity of the Christian lands, and rightfully so. Zengi was thirsty for war. He had correctly assessed the power vacuum that existed in the region and wanted to take full advantage of it.

The Latin kingdoms' efforts to fight against Zengi were very disoriented. At first, Count Raymond II of Tripoli ventured out to meet Zengi's forces in battle while they were besieging Damascene territory. He was defeated, and Zengi now turned his attention toward the Christians. Count Raymond, who lost most of his men in the battle, knew that he would not be able to defeat the Muslims. He approached King Fulk for help.

King Fulk answered the call and marched north with whatever men he could assemble, including a contingent of Templars. His efforts were unsuccessful, though, as he was ambushed by Zengi's forces and forced to retreat to Castle Montferrand in Tripoli. There, Zengi laid siege to the entrapped Christian forces. The situation seemed dire. King Fulk sent messengers to Antioch and Edessa for aid. While the remaining Latin kingdoms started to assemble their armies to help, Fulk managed to negotiate a ransom with the besiegers. In exchange for his and his men's safety, the Christians gave Zengi possession of Castle Montferrand in July of 1137, which further increased his power in the region.

This defeat would demoralize the Christians, although it was a great success for Zengi. Even though Zengi was now in an open war against the Latin kingdoms, he knew that he was much more powerful for one simple reason: the Christians lacked the manpower. That's why he continued to attack the Christian cities in Outremer and took them one by one, eventually reaching Edessa in 1144.

The Christian effort had become even more disjointed by that point. For one thing, King Fulk had passed away in an accident in 1143, and the Kingdom of Jerusalem was left to his young son, Baldwin III, who ruled with his mother, Melisende, since he was not old enough to rule alone. In addition, Joscelin II, Count of Edessa, did not have a good relationship with the rest of the Christian kingdoms. He had been in an alliance with Jerusalem, but the future seemed uncertain after Fulk's death. The young count was not that experienced when it came to military matters, which explains why he was outclassed so much at Edessa.

In late 1144, Joscelin II, who was allied with the Turkish Artuqids, rode out to besiege the city of Aleppo—one of the most important cities Zengi possessed. He left Edessa in the hands of mercenaries, but he was not able to pay them sufficiently for months. This decision would turn out to be fatal for the young count. Knowing that the capital of the county was poorly defended, Zengi besieged the city for a month, building siege equipment and digging under the walls. He finally captured it in December 1144. His armies ravaged the city, massacring soldiers and members of the clergy and selling the women into slavery.

The fall of Edessa was disastrous for the Latin kingdoms. Still, they could not, or did not, send help to Joscelin, who, in a desperate attempt, tried to retake the capital in October 1146. Before that, he ruled the remnants of his county, those that were still untouched by the Muslims. It was a valiant effort by the count, who was acting quickly after Zengi had been murdered in his sleep by a slave. Unfortunately, Joscelin could not recapture the city, as the forces under Zengi's son, Nur ad-Din, drove him out.

Nur ad-Din was Zengi's second son, the self-proclaimed sultan of Aleppo. While similar to his father in his mercilessness, Nur ad-Din was also a devout Muslim. It was his firm belief in Islam that made him wise. He was not like other rulers who indulged themselves in wine and women. Instead, he preferred to spend his time studying the holy texts. Nur ad-Din promoted his wars as holy wars, or jihads, where those who died sacrificed themselves to God or Allah. And even though he had lost some territories to his brother in Iraq, he was eager to recruit experienced mercenaries from every region in the East. Eventually, he bolstered his army so much that he was basically continuing his father's legacy as a threat to be feared. And feared he was.

The Call for the Second Crusade

The situation in Outremer was becoming more and more desperate. The Latin kingdoms had never been as weak since the end of the First Crusade. Edessa, the northernmost kingdom, had fallen almost completely to the Muslims, including the city of Edessa itself. It was not looking too good for the Christians. Thus, when the pilgrims returned to Europe from Outremer with the news of Edessa's fall the next autumn, Pope Eugenius knew that he needed to act quickly. He wanted the Christian kingdoms to venture to the Holy Land once again and help take back Edessa, reinforcing Outremer with fresh warriors from Europe. He wrote to King Louis VII of France, asking him about the possibility of a potential Second Crusade. King Louis saw the journey to Outremer as an opportunity to redeem himself, as he had lost popularity in the eyes of his people when he unrightfully claimed the lands from his Burgundian vassal. The king was excited to hear the pope's concerns and helped him organize a council at Vézelay in the spring of 1146. More importantly, he invited the one man he knew for certain would be in favor of the new Crusade: Bernard of Clairvaux.

The Council of Vézelay proceeded similarly as the Council of Clermont. Everyone knew ahead of the gathering why the pope had called them to assemble. The audience was curious to see Bernard of Clairvaux preach too, as they all remembered his powerful words at Troyes, which had caused the Knights Templar to ascend to unseen levels of popularity. His charisma caused a similar result as what had happened with Pope Urban about fifty years prior. The gathered members of the council were instantly taken up by the idea of going to Outremer to reclaim the lost lands. King Louis and his younger brother Robert were the first ones to vow to venture out. Hundreds soon followed. Many were the descendants of the previous generation that took part in the First Crusade. For those people, it was as much about taking back Edessa and the spiritual salvation that the Second Crusade promised as it was about continuing the legacy of their families and maintaining the prestigious status their fathers had attained. Germany's Conrad III was also convinced to join the Crusade, making it the first time that monarchs of European states led the Crusaders. A group of Crusaders from England would also start their journey to Outremer, but they would divert from their path and end up in Portugal to take part in the *Reconquista*, which we will discuss later.

In late April of the same year, after the news of the new Crusade had spread throughout the continent, the pope and King Louis met at the Paris Temple. The meeting, which had been organized by the new Grand Master of the Knights Templar in France, Everard des Barres, was also attended by about 130 Templars and their sergeants and squires. (Everard would be "officially" elected after the passing of Robert de Craon in Outremer, although the exact date of his death is unknown. Some sources say that Everard held an important role in the order in France, but it is unclear when Everard succeeded Robert.)

The meeting would prove to be vital for both the Templars and the Crusaders. It is thought that this was when the Crusaders received the pope's blessing to wear the iconic red cross on their clothes. The pope would also allow the Templar treasurer to collect taxes from the church to offer financial support to the Crusade. Most importantly, it was decided that Grand Master Everard, with a group of other Templars, was to follow the French army during the Crusade. Over the course of the Crusade, Everard would play a bigger role, becoming, in essence, the military advisor of Louis VII.

The Journey to Outremer

Thus, the two main forces were on their way to Outremer. It has to be said that Conrad III of Germany's forces were not nearly as professional as those of King Louis VII. The biggest factor that determined the overall discipline of the French was the presence of the Knights Templar. King Louis was very impressed by the Templars and their way of life, which they strictly followed. He considered them to be role models for his troops. His trust in the Templars is further shown when he sent Grand Master Everard to the Byzantines to negotiate their passage through Anatolia.

Emperor Manuel Comnenus (Komnenos) was somewhat hesitant to grant the Crusaders military access for two main reasons. Firstly, he had not called for help and did not expect anything for himself should the Crusade be successful, unlike Emperor Alexios in the First Crusade. Secondly, since he was busy fighting in Sicily, he had made peace with the Seljuk Turks and thought that his actions might damage his already-wavering relations with the Muslims. It was due to this that the Byzantine emperor was not liked by the Crusaders.

Matters got worse in November 1147 when the news of Conrad's defeat reached the French forces who had arrived in Nicaea and were planning to cross to the Holy Land. Conrad's army was separated from the French army. In fact, he had reached Constantinople sometime earlier than Louis and had decided to proceed through Anatolia alone. In late October, however, the Germans were ambushed by the Turks at their camp. They were overwhelmed by the light Turkish cavalry, who swarmed their positions. The king and about a tenth of his forces managed to survive and retreat back to the Byzantine territories, but the Germans would partially blame the emperor for not providing military support to the journeying Crusaders.

Conrad and Louis would meet in Nicaea after the disastrous German defeat to discuss how they would continue their march. The two kings decided to take a route that went through the coastline of Anatolia all the way to the port of Antalya. Unfortunately, Conrad soon fell ill and was forced to return to Constantinople; he was only able to reach the Holy Land in 1148.

The route to the Holy Land would prove to be much more problematic to King Louis than to his predecessors in the First Crusade. The French were constantly under attack from the

Turkish forces. Usually, the Turks did not have large numbers. Instead, the Turkish mounted archers quickly harassed the French army, which was moving slowly in a long column from the flanks. It was very difficult for the French to effectively answer the "hit and run" style of the Turks. To reduce the number of casualties and further increase discipline in his forces, King Louis asked Grand Master Everard for his advice. Everard divided the army into smaller contingents that were each led by a Templar. This approach seemed to work; the Crusaders successfully repelled the Turks, first at Ephesus in late December 1147 and then at the valley of Meander, where the Crusaders would be ambushed trying to cross the river but would come out victorious. They even captured a number of the enemy forces.

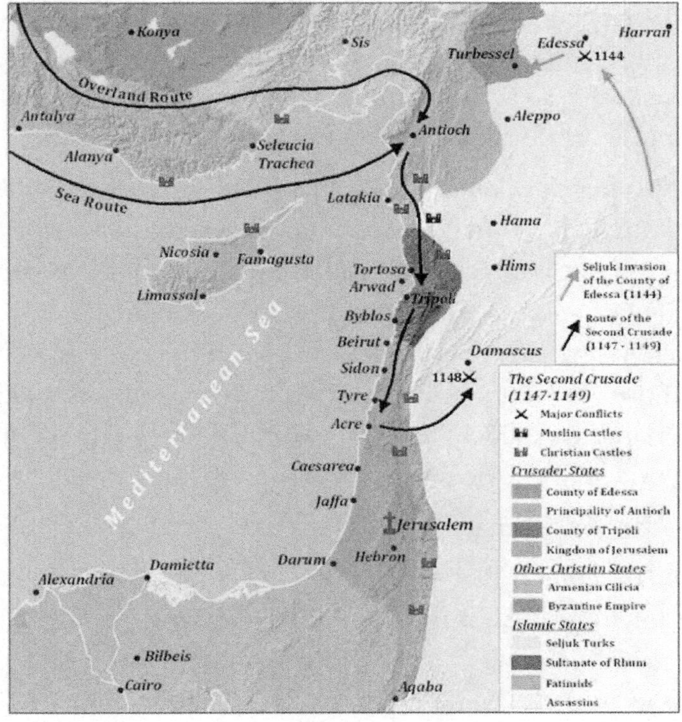

The route of the Second Crusade

CadAPL, CC BY-SA 3.0 https://creativecommons.org/licenses/by-sa/3.0 via Wikimedia Commons https://commons.wikimedia.org/w/index.php?curid=94547884

After Meander, Louis only had to get to the port of Antalya, where he hoped he would be able to transfer the rest of his forces by sea. They would have to endure many difficulties during their final leg of the journey to Antalya, however. At that point, the Crusaders had sparse supplies and not a lot of horses. The heavy cavalry that they did have was of no use in the mountainous regions of southern Anatolia. Thus, as the French passed through the narrow passes of the Cadmus Mountains, they would suffer many casualties from the Turks, who used the terrain to their advantage to constantly harass and disrupt the French forces.

It was at this point that the Templars really showed their military expertise. They understood that the main objective was for the French to get out of the narrow pass and reach Antalya. The Templars started to enforce their discipline harder than before, making the Crusaders follow their lead. The Crusaders developed a deep sense of respect toward the Templars after they managed to up the morale and save Christians from deserting or fleeing.

Finally, after days of struggling, the Crusaders arrived at Antalya. There, with help from the Byzantines, King Louis boarded the ships with his best forces and headed for Port Saint Symeon in the Principality of Antioch. The rest of the forces under the command of the remaining French nobles would soon follow. The rest of the forces, those who did not manage to get on the ships, would have to pass overland to Antioch, and they would almost be fully wiped out by the Turks in the process.

The Fiasco at Damascus

It can be argued that the journey to Antioch was much more difficult for Louis than it was for the First Crusaders. The Crusader army had lost the majority of its forces. In addition, Louis had run out of money, and even if he did have it, what direction the Crusade would go after Antioch was still under question. However, he would receive a lot of help during his stay in Antioch. For one thing, his army got some time to rest after a tiresome and brutal journey.

More importantly, though, Grand Master Everard would step up once again to help the Crusaders, this time financially. As the remaining Crusader forces arrived in Antioch throughout the spring, Everard sailed to Acre, a Templar stronghold. There, he raised the necessary amount to help fund the rest of the expedition. It is logical to assume that Everard got the money directly from the order's treasury, showing, once again, the sheer financial growth the Knights Templar had undergone since their early days. It is also possible that Everard borrowed the money and used the vast riches of the order as insurance.

In any way, Louis was humbled by this action so much that he vowed to repay the Templars as soon as he could, ordering his subjects to raise insane amounts of money for his debts to the order. The French Crown and the Templar Order would become closer than ever after this gracious act from Everard, although he did technically loan the French the money. With this, as well as the pope's decision to entrust many important matters to the Templars in France, the order would basically run the French treasury for the next century and a half.

There was still a question of what was next for the Crusaders. Conrad had finally reached the Holy Land in the spring with the remnants of his force. It was agreed that the plan of action would be decided during an assembly near Acre. Everyone would attend. Alongside the European kings Louis and Conrad, there were the nobility and high-ranking officers of their armies. Young Baldwin III, King of Jerusalem, also attended with his mother, Melisende. The patriarch of Jerusalem was there as well, accompanied by a couple of archbishops from Nazareth and Caesarea. The Knights Templar were also there, represented by Everard, as well as, according to some sources, Robert de Craon, the Grand Master. (Robert is thought to have been still alive by the time of the assembly, but he surely passed away soon after.) Finally, there was the Grand Master of the Knights Hospitaller, Raymond du Puy.

The assembly decided with little to no opposition that the target of the Crusaders should be Damascus. This is a decision that has been frowned upon by modern historians, and for good reason. Damascus's strategic importance is certainly undeniable. So is the fact that the city itself was pretty rich and prosperous, and its surrounding lands were fertile. However, it was also not that wise to attack it then. The Damascenes were Shi'a Muslims, unlike the surrounding Muslim factions, like the one under Nur ad-Din. Thus, the two factions did not really have friendly relations, and the Damascenes had previously sided with the Christians under King Fulk in their efforts to stop Zengi's invasions. Therefore, attacking the only buffer state and a potential ally was not certainly the best idea. Plus, the city itself was heavily guarded, and it was not easy to approach.

Many historians and some contemporaries, like Raymond of Antioch, thought the wiser target was Aleppo—the heart of Nur ad-Din's kingdom—or Edessa, the city that had been lost to the Muslim invaders prior to the Second Crusade. This city was supposed to be the "original target" of the Second Crusade. The main argument that might have overpowered these two options was the fear of Nur ad-Din conquering the city himself. If that happened, he would become the most dominant power in Syria and pose a greater threat to the Latin kingdoms.

Whatever the reasoning was, the target was set, and the Crusaders started preparing. The army was led by the king of Jerusalem, who assembled quite a number of men. King Louis and King Conrad also joined King Baldwin with whatever forces they had left, altogether composing an army of no more than fifty thousand men. It has to be said that the role of the Templars was not as big as in the journey leading up to the final assault on Damascus, although it is safe to assume that they were present in the army. The Crusaders rode out from the coastline through Banias in the summer, arriving near Damascus in late July.

The Crusaders set up camp south of the city in the orchards that bordered it. It was a good location since it provided the attackers with reliable food and water supplies. The orchards were also not that far from the city; they were located about four miles away. On July 24th, the Crusaders started their assault through the orchards. This proved to be a difficult task since the defenders had scattered their vanguard in the trees and had them constantly fire upon the attackers as they advanced. However, this defense was not enough, and the Crusaders managed to successfully go on the offensive and push the majority of the Muslims back to the other side of the Barada River.

There, thanks to the bravery of King Conrad, who fought on foot, and his German troops, the Crusaders overcame the Muslim defenses of the river. They passed over to the other bank and drove them all the way back to the city. Then, they started to use the wood found in the orchards to build palisades and siege equipment. It all seemed dire for the Damascenes until relief forces arrived in the city. Unur, the ruler of Damascus, had called for help from the atabeg of Mosul and Nur ad-Din. By the time the Crusaders had crossed the river, the Damascenes had assembled enough reinforcements for a counterattack, which halted the progress of the Christians.

Still, since the beginning of the siege, the Crusaders were pretty successful. However, for some reason, the attackers would make the fatal mistake of abandoning their position at the orchards and moving the camp to the eastern side of the city on the plains. There is no real explanation for this. It was a foolish move for many reasons, including the scarcity of supplies at the new camp. When the defenders realized that the Crusaders had moved, they sent reinforcements to the orchards, where they built barricades and mounted more defenses, making it impossible for the attackers to return to their original camp. The Damascenes knew that the Crusaders had made a mistake and did not really force a fight upon them, especially once they knew that even more help from Nur ad-Din was on the way.

The Crusaders understood that they had put themselves at a massive disadvantage and that they needed to act quickly before they ran out of food and water and before the defenders would get new forces. The Crusaders decided to abandon the siege and retreated on July 28th, just five days after their arrival. Their shameful retreat was accompanied by constant harassment from the Muslim forces, which followed the Crusaders as far as they could, inflicting many casualties.

The failure to capture Damascus was catastrophic. Not only was it demoralizing for the Latin kingdoms, which knew their position in the region had weakened, but it was also a disaster for the rest of the Christian world. The Second Crusade was a complete fiasco from start to finish, as the Crusaders were unable to achieve anything of importance. This is why, after Damascus, the different parties started blaming each other to justify their loss. For some, the failed siege at Damascus was the fault of local Christian barons, who were known for making deals with the Muslims. When discussing who would be put in charge of Damascus once it was taken, the local barons had completely been left out, leaving some to suspect that they had conspired with the Muslims, giving them information ahead of time. Others thought that Raymond of Antioch's unwillingness to support the Crusaders led to their failure. Raymond, unlike the others, did not support the assault on Damascus. All in all, there is a lot of speculation as to whose fault the failure at Damascus really was.

Later sources also partially put the blame on the Templars. A couple of German monks who traveled to Outremer in the 1160s wrote that the order was to blame for the fiasco of the Second Crusade. They accused the Templars of conspiring against the Christians, even saying that they were paid by the Damascenes not only for information but also for the deliberate sabotage or disruption of the Crusaders' ranks.

These and other accusations toward the order have never actually been proven, however. What is clear is the fact that the Templars played an influential role in the Second Crusade. King Louis trusted the brothers very much, and the Templars helped increase the discipline and professionalism of the army. Plus, we should not forget about the funding that the Templars raised for the Crusaders after their arrival in the Holy Land. During the Second Crusade, the Templars were involved in events in Iberia. There, the Crusader forces would join the Spanish and the Portuguese in the *Reconquista.*

The Iberian Crusade

Along with their role in the main Crusader campaign, the Templars would also see some action in Iberia during the Second Crusade. It is important to remember that the Second Crusade, despite being caused by the loss of Edessa in Outremer, did not really serve its original purpose. After the arrival of the Franco-German forces in the Holy Land, the Crusaders did not even try to recapture Edessa or engage in defensive warfare. Instead, they chose to expand the Christian territories with their assault on Damascus, which failed miserably. All in all, it was a disjointed effort, with wars being fought in three different regions in the name of the Crusade.

The first, as we already discussed, was the main campaign in Outremer. The other two were the so-called Wendish Crusade, where the northern European Crusaders ventured out against the Slavs, and the Crusade in Iberia as part of the *Reconquista.* Due to the involvement of the Templars in the latter, we shall focus on the Crusader efforts in Spain and Portugal, which were rather successful.

By the time the Second Crusade was called, the *Reconquista* had been well underway, with the Iberian kingdoms seeing more and more success in driving the Muslims out of the peninsula. The Knights Templar was an established organization in both Spain and Portugal by then, with the brothers being in possession of dozens of fortresses to aid in their fight against the Moors. In a way, the *Reconquista* was already an unofficial Crusade, but the actual Crusaders would get involved in the fight until sometime in 1147.

This group of Crusaders set sail from the British Isles, planning to circle the continent and arrive at the Holy Land by sea instead of crossing the English Channel to France and going overland. Consisting of warriors from England and Scotland, as well as parts of northern France, Germany, Flanders, and Frisia, the Crusaders started their journey from Dartmouth in May of 1147. This group did not have a monarch or a prince to lead it, which was different from the main forces under Louis and Conrad. Instead, different groups would be led by different counts and barons, like Arnout IV of Aarschot leading the German contingent and Hervey de Glanvill of Suffolk leading the Crusaders from England. Still, it was a pretty sizeable force of about two hundred ships.

The Crusaders landed at Porto in June of 1147. It is logical to assume that they were forced to stop in Portugal due to bad weather and to resupply before they continued their journey to Outremer. However, contemporary developments in the Christian world also have some historians convinced that the Crusaders came to Iberia to assist the Spanish and the Portuguese in the *Reconquista*. It is believed that Bernard of Clairvaux motivated these groups from the Low Countries to come to the aid of the Iberian Christians. Also, Pope Eugene had given his blessings to King Alfonso VII of León-Castile in his efforts against the Muslims, basically authorizing the Crusade in Iberia. Previously, Pope Paschal II had told the Iberians that their fight against the Muslims served the same purpose as the Crusaders' efforts in the Holy Land, giving the *Reconquista* the status of a holy war. Thus, if Bernard and Pope Eugene planned for a part of the Crusader forces to journey to Iberia to help against the

Moors, the Second Crusade can be seen as a general holy war on all non-Christians.

Whatever it was that made the northern European Crusaders land at Porto, they would prove to be of great help against the Muslims. After their arrival, the Crusaders quickly met with Alfonso I of Portugal (who was technically not a king at the time). With the help of the Templars, Alfonso had already managed to expand his territories and drive the Muslims out. At the meeting, the two parties discussed a potential offensive on Lisbon, which was one of the richest and most important cities in Iberia. The Crusaders were initially reluctant to participate. This was because they knew of the previously failed siege of Lisbon, which had taken place in 1142. However, after much discussion, they agreed. In return, Alfonso promised them much of the loot from the city, as well as lands and exemption from taxes in the conquered territories.

The Siege of Lisbon. By Joaquim Rodrigues Braga - Joaquim Rodrigues Braga
https://commons.wikimedia.org/w/index.php?curid=1596202

The combined forces of the Crusaders and the Portuguese laid siege to Lisbon on July 1st. There was a total of about twenty thousand men, including a contingent of Templars who had become regulars in the Portuguese armies. At the time, Lisbon was thought to have had a population of about 150,000 people, many of them refugees from Santarém and other newly conquered Portuguese towns near the River Tagus. Unlike their hasty approach at Damascus, the Crusaders decided to wait and blockade the city. Eventually, after four months, the Moors surrendered in late October due to the lack of supplies in the city, which had caused a mass famine.

The capture of the city was relatively peaceful, with the Christians allowing the civilians to leave after they entered. The capture of Lisbon would be a pivotal victory for the *Reconquista.* The victory solidified the Portuguese position against the Muslims and swung the balance of power in favor of the Christians. It was also one of the more significant victories for the Crusaders during the Second Crusade, especially since they did not really achieve anything of importance in Outremer.

The Aftermath of the Second Crusade

Overall, the Second Crusade was not nearly as successful as the first one. The main campaign had failed, and the victory in Iberia was the only silver lining. However, the Templars' role throughout the whole Crusade cannot be understated. The Second Crusade boosted the popularity and status of the Templars even more. Because of their close involvement with King Louis's army, they gained much respect in France, playing a significant role in France's financial affairs. The funds the Templars managed to assemble after the Crusaders' arrival at Outremer also show the power they had accumulated since their creation. Many Crusaders who stayed in the Holy Land and Iberia would join the Templar Order and reside in one of their numerous castles as sergeants or squires. The Templars sought to build on their successful participation in the Second Crusade. They were looking at a bright future ahead of them, and what followed was a period where they were at the height of their power, as they were regarded as the most respected organization in the Christian world.[7]

[7] Napier, G. (2011). *The Rise and Fall of the Knights Templar.* History Press. Chapter 4.

Hill, P. (2018). *The Knights Templar at War, 1120–1312.* Pen & Sword Military.

Forey, A. (2004). "The Siege of Lisbon and the Second Crusade." *Portuguese Studies*, 20, 1–13. http://www.jstor.org/stable/41105214.

Martin, S. (2011). *The Knights Templar.* Oldcastle Books. Chapter 2.

Constable, G. (1953). "The Second Crusade as Seen by Contemporaries." *Traditio*, 9, 213–279. http://www.jstor.org/stable/27830277.

Part Two – The Rise of The Knights Templar

Chapter 5 – The Rich Knights of Christ

We have already covered the origin story of the Knights Templar. The order became much more than a brotherhood of nine knights who pledged to protect the pilgrims traveling to the Holy Land. From the creation of the order in the early 12th century up to the Second Crusade, the whole Christian world got to know what the Templars stood for. Starting from the second half of the 1100s, the Templars slowly rose to the peak of their power, expanding the order all over the continent. This chapter looks to explore a different side of the Templars, one that is often forgotten, as it is often overshadowed by their warrior monk lifestyle.

Rags to Riches

The official name of the Knights Templar is technically the Order of the Poor Knights of Christ and the Temple of Solomon. As we have remarked many times, the word "poor" did not accurately reflect the order's status. The Templars were becoming more and more popular, which meant there were more and more of those who wanted to donate. And although the brothers followed a strict Benedictine lifestyle, they were in possession of a small kingdom's worth of wealth. This fact would be recognized by the Christian world soon enough.

One of the pivotal moments in the process of the order's establishment as a fully-fledged, strong financial institution was the Second Crusade. After the arrival of King Louis's forces in Outremer, Grand Master Everard would singlehandedly raise enough money for the campaign to continue. Funding a whole Crusade was not an easy task; in fact, many rulers would decide not to take part in the Crusades because of the massive costs associated with it. However, Everard managed to gather all the money needed for an expedition to Damascus for about fifty thousand men, either getting it directly from Templar reserves or borrowing it and using Templar possessions as insurance. While it is not known how he raised money, it is believed that Everard gave King Louis about thirty thousand French livres and two thousand marks of silver. Of course, this was a loan; the Templar Grand Master did not simply gift the French king this much money. If Everard had been kind enough to gift the king this huge sum, Louis would surely have been embarrassed.

The Templars' financial involvement in France was also boosted by the pope's initiative for the members of the order to become treasurers of the state. This tradition, which would evolve over time, would continue for more than a century and a half until the complete demise of the Templars. The order operating from the Paris Temple, which was the headquarters of the Templars not only in France but also unofficially in mainland Europe, would be in charge of the French treasury. They would do everything from collecting taxes to giving out loans. They assisted the French monarchs in financial matters and did so pretty effectively. For instance, they helped Philip II restructure the tax collection system and significantly increased his overall revenue. After Louis VII, the French kings would select one of the Templars to serve the throne for their lifetime. This allowed the monarch to form a close relationship with the order, which was not only limited to financial advice.

The system the Templars pioneered was much like a modern bank. Banks did not exist in Europe back then, making it even more impressive how neatly the order was able to handle the different fiscal issues. Perhaps their general devotion to order and discipline, which was, in turn, based on the Benedictine lifestyle, helped the Templars establish one of the first and most effective early banking systems in Europe. For example, the Templars realized there were a lot of people in different locations willing to borrow money from the order or deposit their possessions in their hands. So, they came up with a credit note system. When a person deposited money to a Templar location, they would be given a special official document with the details of the transaction. This document could be redeemed at any other Templar site with no additional costs or difficulties. In the meantime, before the deposited money was taken out, the order could loan to another party or use it to invest in its own development, as the knights were confident that it would be returned because of the influx of money the

order saw on a regular basis. This system would last until the order disbanded, and various individuals, from European nobles to members of the Catholic Church, would use it regularly. The Templars would be open for business on most days, and they usually agreed with their clients about the transaction details beforehand.

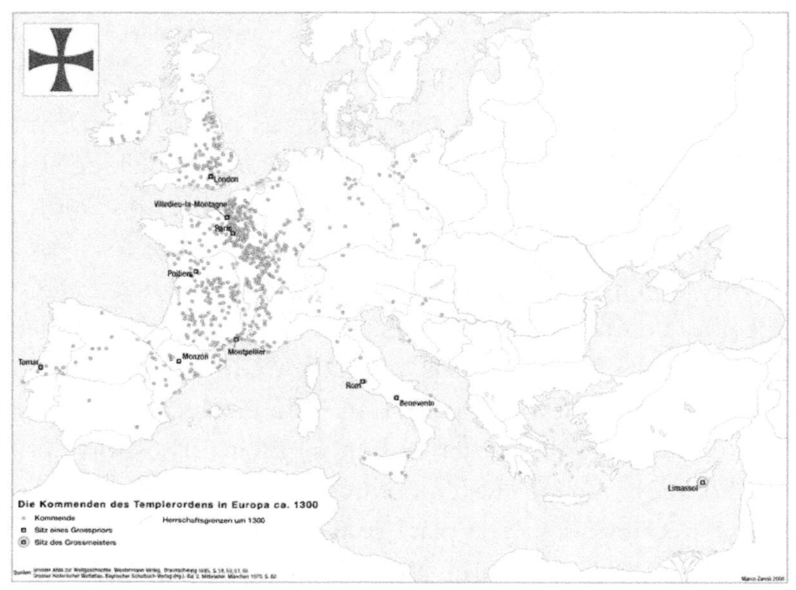

Templar holdings in Europe

Marco Zanoli, CC BY-SA 4.0 <https://creativecommons.org/licenses/by-sa/4.0>, via Wikimedia Commons https://commons.wikimedia.org/wiki/File:Templerorden_in_Europa_1300.png

In their financial endeavors in Europe, the Knights Templar would see a lot of support from the papacy. By the time the Templars started implementing their convenient fiscal system, different popes had already shown how much they valued the order; the papal bulls are perhaps the best example of this. They also made the Grand Master of the Templar Order one of the most powerful men in all of the Christian world by giving him the privilege of "directly answering" to the pope and not any other monarch or lord. Because of the close relationship between two of the most respected organizations in all of Christianity, the papacy would use the services provided by the order just as much as lords from different kingdoms.

In the early 1160s, the Templars were performing a similar role for Pope Alexander III as they had in France; they effectively managed the papacy's treasury. Most of the papacy's financial matters would see the involvement of the Templars in one way or another. For example, Pope Innocent III heavily relied on the

Templars when he tried to raise funds for the Fourth Crusade, which began in 1202. Not only did the pope directly borrow from the Order and later repay his loans, but once he had the opportunity, he also gave the Templars additional privileges of collecting taxes from members of the clergy to better organize the upcoming war effort. The Templars, along with the Knights Hospitaller, were responsible for transferring the actual funds to the Holy Land during the Crusade, as well as dealing with all of the fiscal issues that might have arisen during the process. This way, the Knights Templar continued to further cement itself as the biggest and most influential Christian organization after the papacy.

Financial Ties with the English Crown

The role of the Templars as (proto) bankers would increase in Europe as time went by. Besides their main center of operations at the Paris Temple, they would be very successful in the British Isles. They even started to conduct business with the British Crown itself. The Templars' involvement with fiscal matters in England and the whole of Europe can be attributed to increasing levels of globalization, which was accelerated by the events of the 12th century.

At the time, more and more European kingdoms began to emerge as sovereign states with clearly defined territories. Due to this, the importance of international trade began to rise. The development of the concept of mercantilism was also a contributing factor, as wealth slowly shifted from the hands of the feudal lords (who, by all means, still held the majority of resources) into the hands of merchants, traders, farmers, and people of other professions. These people were more willing to contribute to the building of markets and roads, which bolstered their income even more. They paid more taxes to their rulers, with the money then being reinvested to increase the economic landscapes in which they all coexisted. It was all a big chain reaction, and the Templars managed to find their own niche in the developing world.

England was one of the most progressive and economically advanced places in Europe at the time. It was only natural for the Templars to find their footing there. This would play into the formation of England as an economic power and London, therefore, as an economic hub. Starting in the late 12th century, English people from all social classes are documented as having deposited their possessions at the London Temple. Again, people would entrust the order with everything from actual currency to pots of gold and silver to other miscellaneous valuable items. The order's temples were one of the safest places at the time to keep one's money. They had been built by clever engineers, and all of them were designed as fortifications. Most of them were even designed to have secret passes and keeps underground. They were also well guarded by tens, if not hundreds, of knights, squires, and sergeants.

Another prominent reason, as already partially discussed above, was the convenience of the transactions. The client was able to confidently leave their possessions in the hands of the Templars with the ability to retrieve them from any Templar location at any time without too many complications. The people felt respect for the order, which made the organization trustworthy. And not even kings (in most cases) would dare to mess with an internationally well-respected and sacred institution. The order essentially guaranteed safety, security, and secrecy, and as the records show, the English rulers saw its importance from the very start.

On many occasions, different kings would use the riches of the temples to their own advantage, as they were aware of the availability of funds. In times of need, they would take large amounts of money from the Templars and repay the order over time from other treasuries of the state, such as Westminster or the Tower of London. In 1276, Edward I would withdraw one thousand marks. Henry III would seize forty thousand marks from the temple as a way to confiscate the money from Falkes de Bréauté, a Norman adventurer who entrusted the money to the Templars but was then accused of treachery and conspiracy. One of the most popular ways for kings to repay the Templars was by granting them all sorts of additional privileges, like exemption of different kinds of taxes or providing help to the order in building new holdings.

Thus, the Knights Templar was seen as a reliable financial institution in England. In turn, this accumulated a similar sense of trust between the order and the English Crown. Members of the order were often employed by the English monarchs to oversee a myriad of fiscal issues, such as the collection of taxes. They were not only limited to conducting private business in the name of the Templars. Instead, they were made official ambassadors of the Crown and assigned to different missions. For example, a group of Templars would oversee the transportation of money from England to Ireland. In exchange, the English rulers agreed to pay for any injuries on the road or reimburse them for their troubles. The Templars also acted as third-party trustees. The most notable example of this was when they were entrusted with the ownership of castles that were supposed to be a part of a dowry from Louis VII's daughter to Henry II's son during their arranged marriage. Because the two kings agreed to marry their children when they were still very young, the castles went into the Templars' possession until the children were old enough to marry and, thus, receive them.

These and a dozen more fiscal services were performed by the Knights Templar on a regular basis in England from the late 12th to the end of the 13th century. They were effectively the best financial institution in the kingdom until the wealthy Italian merchant organizations became more prominent in Europe. The English monarchs trusted the Templars on many occasions, and the Templars never disappointed. They continued to carry out different sorts of transactions for the Crown for more than a year and earned an amicable reputation with the English kings. The Templars not only ensured the safety of the funds but were also very flexible in their agreements, developing the first fully-functioning banking system in Europe. The Templars' ways of handling money so effectively, as well as their integrity and administrative capacity, are certainly impressive. It certainly helped send the Templars to the height of their power.

New Holdings

Perhaps one of the best indications of the Templars' rise to power was the extensive number of new holdings they either received or built during the second half of the 12th century. Of course, the order had several headquarters in different regions, which were both the most fortified and the richest. However, the Templars also built countless buildings that served a myriad of purposes. For example, they built churches, mills, and bridges. With time, they also extended whatever they had already acquired. For example, by the 1170s, the Templars are thought to have expanded their main holding at the time, the former Al-Aqsa Mosque at Mount Temple. They completely renovated the old building and added new underground vaults and halls, where they allegedly kept their most precious possessions.

Other castles in Outremer also received love from the order. In fact, it is estimated that the Templars spent the most money and resources on their architectural projects, either repairing those castles and fortresses or building completely new holdings. These castles were heavily guarded since they were located at various strategic points all over Jordan and Palestine. Most of their walls were over 150 feet high and accompanied by a set of defensive towers at every possible point. The costs associated with maintaining, let alone building, such grand structures are truly remarkable, especially when we take into account that they were always manned by hundreds of soldiers.

The Templar fortresses of Outremer were so big that they had the capability of sheltering thousands of people in case they were ever driven out of their towns during an invasion. The Templars had stocked the castles with more weapons than the garrison needed, as well as food and other provisions for potential sieges. The impressive Templar holdings of the East include Atlit Castle, also known as Pilgrim Castle, on the northern coast of Israel; it was built during the Fifth Crusade and capable of supporting about forty thousand soldiers during a siege. Near Antioch, the order was in possession of the famous Baghras (Bagras) Castle, renamed Gaston by the Templars. It was initially abandoned by the Byzantines but repaired and used by the order. Alongside these, the order was in control of Acre, Jaffa, and Sidon, which were all heavily fortified and of great importance.

Castle Almourol

Daniel Feliciano, CC BY-SA 2.5 https://creativecommons.org/licenses/by-sa/2.5 via Wikimedia Commons https://commons.wikimedia.org/w/index.php?curid=638069

Iberia was another region where most of the Templar holdings were giant castles. Perhaps the reason behind this was the existence of an imminent threat: the Muslims. After all, they were present both in Outremer and Iberia. Just like in the Holy Land, the Templars would be granted a lot of their fortresses. In fact, it can be argued that the order was more favored by the Iberian lords than by their Latin counterparts in the East due to the number of holdings they donated to the Templars. The Castle of Soure was the first one to be awarded to them, and by the 1170s, other Portuguese castles, such as Almourol and Longroiva, would also be in their possession.

Out of these two, the Castle of Almourol, situated on a rocky island in the Tagus River Valley, was heavily damaged when the order got hold of it. However, the Templars repaired and extended the castle, adding ten additional defensive towers and a more fortified inner keep.

The Master of the Templar Order in Portugal at the time, Gualdim Pais, also personally oversaw the construction of two more castles, Pombal and Tomar, with the latter becoming the Portuguese headquarters of the Knights Templar. In Spain, alongside the six major castles the order received from King Alfonso's will, the Templars possessed Miravet, one of the best fortresses in all of Iberia. Despite the fact that the later lords of Aragon and Castile were more favorable toward the Knights Hospitaller and not as gracious toward the Templars, the order managed to hold on to their precious possessions until it met its demise. The Knights Templar continued to play a major role in the *Reconquista* and was a force to be reckoned with in Iberia.

Of course, Templar holdings were not only heavily fortified and strategically important castles. In most of Europe, Templars were in charge of churches, monastery complexes, a variety of agricultural and industrial buildings, and sometimes even small towns. Despite the fact that the Templars had several big castles, the absence of a direct threat and a potential enemy meant the Templars were not needed to man these huge fortresses, unlike in the Holy Land or Iberia. Instead, to show their gratitude, European lords became more and more creative when they granted the order new possessions. The Templars would proudly take over whatever lands they could and make the most of them. Over time, as more members joined the Knights Templar, the skills of the order also increased, which meant they were perfectly capable of conducting agricultural or industrial processes and competent enough to run small towns.

The Templars were already established after their initial visit to Europe in 1127, as they had received enough estates through donations from different European lords. Later on, these estates, which mostly comprised of farms or manors, would be grown to include a network of Templar-built houses, from where the brothers would collect taxes and fund future expansion efforts. These became known as preceptories, which were subordinate houses and communities of the Knights Templar.

One of the main reasons behind the Templars' enthusiasm for building was their relationship with the secretive medieval and now-famous guild of the Masons. In fact, there seems to have been a special unit composed of the brothers, who were a separate class of "Templar Masons." Nowadays, the guild of the Masons is often associated with secret societies and conspiracy theories. Even though most of it is made up, it is true that the members of the guild did not like the involvement of outside parties in their affairs. Even so, they could be easily identified due to the use of excessive geometric shapes in their buildings.

The Paris Temple can be considered one of the most focal examples. It was built in the 12th century by the order and served as its main headquarters in Europe. Although the Paris Temple was demolished in the 19th century by Napoleon, it was described as having tall walls with corner towers and sharp edges, resembling the work of the Templar Masons. While the Templar architecture of the time was still confined to Benedictine standards—without any complex ornaments and details—it was still very unique compared to everything else from the period. We shall return to the matter of potential Templar involvement with the guild of the Masons later on.[8]

[8] Martin, S. (2011). *The Knights Templar.* Oldcastle Books. Chapter 2.

Ferris, E. (1902). "The Financial Relations of the Knights Templars to the English Crown." *The American Historical Review,* 8 (1), 1-17.

Hill, P. (2018). *The Knights Templar at War, 1120-1312.* Pen & Sword Military. Part 2.

Faith, J. (2011). *The Knights Templar in Somerset.* History Press.

Napier, G. (2011). *The Rise and Fall of the Knights Templar.* History Press.

Chapter 6 – Templar Military Power in the Holy Land

The Second Crusade ended terribly for the Crusaders. The kings of Europe had invested a lot into their eastward campaigns, but they ultimately failed to achieve any sort of meaningful progress in Outremer. The Second Crusade, however, as we have already remarked, was not as disastrous for the Knights Templar. In the years following the Second Crusade, the Templars' military involvement in the Holy Land would only increase. This chapter will explore further military endeavors of the Templars in the East and how its successes and sometimes failures put the Knights Templar at the height of their power.

Following the Second Crusade

In a way, the failure of the Second Crusade increased the need for a stronger Christian presence in the Holy Land. Edessa was completely destroyed, and those Latin kingdoms that remained were not really in a position to challenge the supremacy of the Muslims on their own. Therefore, the years that followed the Second Crusade would be crucial in determining the future of Christianity in Outremer.

As we have already mentioned, it is not exactly clear when Everard des Barres officially became the Grand Master of the Templars. His heavy involvement in the Second Crusade was more than enough proof of his competence as a reliable and experienced leader. Over the course of the campaign, his expertise bailed the Crusaders out of what would have been doomed situations, such as when he reorganized the French army to increase morale and discipline to pass through Anatolia or when he singlehandedly raised enough money for the continuation of the Crusade in Outremer. He was already a well-known and respected figure during the Crusaders' council near Acre, probably hinting at the fact that he was the de-facto Grand Master of the Templar Order by then. Robert de Craon, the second Grand Master of the Templar and the successor to Hugues de Payens, is thought to have passed away in January 1149. It is believed that this was the time when Everard was officially elected as the new Grand Master.

However, instead of staying in the Holy Land, which was the typical dwelling place for the Grand Master, Everard chose to return to France with King Louis. The reason behind this might be the prestige he had accumulated during the Crusade with the king, as well as his nostalgia and love of his home. In any case, he left André de Montbard, one of the nine founding knights of the order and an equally experienced and competent leader, in charge. Around 1150, Everard, as the Grand Master of the Templars, received a letter in France from André, who requested reinforcements and additional funds for the well-being of the order.

There was another much more concerning point made in André's letter. The Second Crusade had somehow managed to increase the Muslim threat instead of diminishing it. Nur ad-Din was on an absolute rampage, having established firm control over all of Syria, and he had his eyes fixed on the Latin kingdoms. After Edessa, Antioch was his next target, and Raymond, Prince of Antioch, knew it. He had seen initial success in repelling Nur ad-

Din, but as time went by, the situation seemed more and more dire for Antioch.

Due to Raymond's somewhat poor relationship with the rest of the Latin kingdoms, he had allied with the Kurdish Assassins in a desperate effort to stop the sultan's advance. It was all in vain. Nur ad-Din ran over Antioch, defeating the alliance first at Baghras and then at Inab. Eventually, the Muslims ambushed Raymond's camp in late June 1149, slaying the prince and destroying the majority of Antioch's forces in one night. It was a sweeping victory for Nur ad-Din, who cut Raymond's head off. He sent it to his rival, the caliph of Baghdad.

Nur ad-Din's success was a signal for the Christians to unify. Responding to the letter from the patriarch of Antioch, André de Montbard assembled more than a thousand Templars and Templar squires to join King Baldwin of Jerusalem's relief force. Although the army was, in theory, not large enough to defeat Nur ad-Din in a head-to-head battle, their quick response to the call and appearance in the north forced the Muslims to negotiate. In the treaty, most of Antioch's lands were seized by Nur ad-Din, but it was the best the Christians could manage. At least they had avoided a complete collapse of the principality and had hope that, as time went by, their chances of fighting back would increase.

Help did arrive in the form of Everard des Barres and other Templars sometime in late 1151 or early 1152. However, after his return to Outremer, Everard resigned from the position of Grand Master, choosing to return to France, where he appears to have joined the Cistercians at Clairvaux, living the rest of his days as a monk. Bernard de Tremelay was elected as the new Grand Master, who, despite his short time as the head of the order, was pretty successful. Most notably, in 1152, the forces of Jerusalem somehow managed to defeat a much larger invading Artuqid Turkish force that had camped close to the Holy City. In a miraculous victory, the Christians slew five thousand Muslims, giving them some much-needed good news. While the victory over the Artuqids was not as significant in the grand scheme of things, it was still a motivating factor for the Christians. It eventually resulted in their rally and a new war effort in Egypt.

The Siege of Ascalon

Ascalon was one of the most important cities in the East. It was located on the Palestinian coast of the Mediterranean, and it was surrounded by Christian-controlled lands from all sides. The Kingdom of Jerusalem controlled the lands on its north and east, while the Templars were in charge of Gaza, some ten miles south of the city. The order had received the area as a gift in 1149/1150, and it spent many resources in building the deserted Gaza into one of the most well-defended strongholds in all of Outremer. The Templars had reconstructed the destroyed lands and fortified Gaza beyond belief. In fact, the order had established such a firm position in Gaza and the southeastern areas of Ascalon that the Egyptians had given up trying to reinforce the city. While the Egyptians had tried to take Gaza back due to its importance in their access to Ascalon, the Templars had defended their fortress with much enthusiasm, impressing even William of Tyre, one of the most vocal critics of the Knights Templar.

Nevertheless, Ascalon was still a very difficult place to attack. The fact that it was deep in the Christian territories meant the Egyptians had to make quite an effort over the years to supply it with weapons, provisions, and men. It was surrounded by thick stone walls and had multiple towers, which were always manned by the defenders. Still, the victory over the Artuqids near Jerusalem, when paired with the rise of King Baldwin III from the shadow of his mother, Melisende, as the legitimate king of Jerusalem, as well as the fact that the Templar efforts had decreased the Fatimid presence in the region, gave the Christians the confidence to organize an attack on Ascalon.

Baldwin III called for reinforcements from all over his kingdom, and his call was sufficiently answered. Of course, Templar Grand Master Bernard de Tremelay and the Grand Master of the Knights Hospitaller, Raymond du Puy, were there with whatever brothers they could assemble for the siege. In addition to the military orders, most of the Jerusalem nobility were present with their smaller forces. The united force arrived at Ascalon in January 1153 and camped outside the city. During their march, they witnessed the Fatimid settlers who lived outside of the city walls retreating back to the fortress. This made the Christians' journey relatively smooth without any real complications.

The siege was also accompanied by a naval blockade, led by Gerard of Sidon, who commanded fifteen ships and patrolled the seas. This fleet did not allow resources to reach Ascalon or let anyone flee from the city. In addition to this, new reinforcements would be received in the form of pilgrims who arrived in the Holy Land by sea during Easter. King Baldwin offered to pay those who wished to join the siege and bought some of their ships to dismantle and construct more siege equipment.

The siege of Ascalon continued for five months. The attackers tried to stall the siege for as long as they could, hoping to starve the defenders out and force them to give up. By then, only small skirmishes had been carried out between the two sides, and King Baldwin wanted to minimize his casualties as much as he could. However, a sizeable Egyptian fleet would eventually arrive to relieve Ascalon, carrying about seventy galleys' worth of supplies and men. The massive Egyptian fleet met with little resistance from the blockading Christian fleet under Gerard of Sidon, who correctly realized that his forces would have been defeated in all-out naval combat and retreated.

Still, despite this, the Christians were seeing some progress. They had managed to move closer to the city and were slowly advancing. The defenders tried to harass the sieging troops with arrows and pieces of debris they would light on fire, but they did not see any significant success. Finally, in August, a part of the city's wall collapsed, as it had been under constant bombardment from Baldwin's forces. Suddenly, the attackers had an opening. Grand Master Bernard realized this and rushed to the gap with a small force of forty Templars, which was separated from the rest of the attacking forces. The Templars tried to advance by themselves without help from the main army, and while they did manage to get inside the walls, they were eventually cut down by the defending forces. This somewhat careless move cost Bernard his life, and the bodies of the dead Templars were hung from the city walls to intimidate the Christians.

However, Baldwin was convinced that his armies were still in a commanding position. A breach had been made, and the attackers were not about to give up after five months of slow progress. Instead, they retreated for a day and held a council, where they decided to continue the attack. Instead of using the breach to enter the city, the attackers continued to bombard Ascalon, forcing the defenders to surrender about a week later, on August 22nd, 1153. Baldwin agreed to let the Muslims leave in peace, and he proudly entered the city. He entrusted its governance to his brother Amalric. This marked one of the biggest victories of the Latin kingdoms in Outremer.

The Templars' peculiar move during the siege has been explained by different historians. Some, like William of Tyre, believed that the Grand Master and his small squad wanted to be the first ones to loot whatever parts of the city they could. They underestimated the strength of the defenders. According to William, the Templars knew that if a full-on assault was ordered by Baldwin, his men would pillage whatever was the most valuable in Ascalon. He essentially attributes their action to their innate greed. Other records are similar, but they do not really blame the Templars for being motivated by their own gains. Instead, other chronicles say that the Templars managed to make an impressive push toward the city's center but were eventually cut off and slain deep inside the city. Some even tell of the treachery of those nobles who accompanied the Templars but refused to follow them inside the city. In any case, the Grand Master's hasty decision mostly likely caused the contingent of Templars to be separated from the main army, which was not under the command of Bernard, unlike his knights. Whatever the truth may be, Ascalon was still a success for the Christians, meaning that it was also a success for the Templar Order in the long run.

Nur-ad Din's Retaliation

The years following the siege of Ascalon saw a shift in the balance of power in the East. While Baldwin III successfully captured the last of the Fatimid cities in the Holy Land, the Muslim states continued to mobilize. Not one year had passed since the capture of Ascalon before Nur ad-Din laid siege to Damascus, a city whose value we have already remarked upon. By then, the Damascene leaders, afraid of Nur ad-Din's might, had allied with the Latin kingdoms on a couple of occasions, thinking that their alliance would be an effective deterrent. Still, Nur ad-Din seized the city relatively easily in just a week with help from the inside, and even though he returned to Aleppo with his forces, taking Damascus was one more step closer to the doorstep of the Christian Holy Land.

With Damascus under his belt, Nur ad-Din and the Christians continued to stare each other down, and a series of skirmishes would break out here and there, although they were mostly smaller raids. Surprisingly, the Templars would be pretty involved in these conflicts, patrolling different trade routes and attacking hostile Muslim caravans that wished to cut their path short by entering the Holy Land. The Templars would not only disturb the travelers but also often take their valuables to add to their own treasures, further increasing their riches. Most notably, the Templars struck gold when they managed to capture a wanted Egyptian outcast vizier and his son, who were trying to flee to Cairo during a period of instability in Egypt. In fact, the vizier and his son had conspired against the caliph and were charged with the murder of the caliph's brothers. Unfortunately for them, they were ambushed by a contingent of Templars, who slew the vizier and sold his son to the Egyptians for sixty thousand pieces of gold.

In May 1157, Nur ad-Din would continue his advance with an assault on Castle Banias, which was controlled by Humphrey of Toron. This happened because King Baldwin III had violated an agreement that had previously been reached by the Christians and Nur ad-Din by ordering a raid on some Turkish-occupied areas in the region. Humphrey and a contingent of Knights Hospitaller, who dwelled in Banias after the castle had been granted to them by Baldwin some time beforehand, managed to hold out for as long as they could. They fought valiantly while waiting for relief forces from the king. After hearing that Baldwin's cavalry was on its way, Nur ad-Din decided to abandon the siege and instead raze Banias to the ground before retreating.

In fact, Baldwin's vanguard just missed the Muslim forces that were ordered to fall back. The king's army decided to camp by a nearby lake, but the men were as careless as ever, thinking that Nur ad-Din had gone all the way back to Damascus. The Muslims ambushed the Christian camp, running over the unorganized forces, which could not mobilize amid the attack. While Baldwin himself managed to escape, Nur ad-Din's forces captured a lot of prisoners, including Templar Grand Master Bertrand de Blanchefort (who had succeeded André de Montbard) and the future Grand Master Odo of Saint-Amand. The latter would be released in March 1159, while Bertrand was ransomed by the Byzantine emperor in May of that year. After their defeat at Banias, Bertrand added new points to the Latin Rule of the Templars that talked about discipline during camping while on a mission.

This defeat at the hands of Nur ad-Din was disastrous for King Baldwin III. As for the Templars, while their reaction to the absence of the Grand Master is not known, they seem to have continued existing as before, staying true to the hierarchy of the order and answering to the brother who was now in charge. Still, it seems that they were more reserved when it came to making big decisions, such as going to war in Baldwin's army between 1157 and 1159. They were absent in the Battle of Butaiha, for example, which ended in a victory for the Christians.

Baldwin III died in February of 1162 and was succeeded by his younger brother, Amalric, the one who had been granted the city of Ascalon after the Christians' triumph against the Fatimids. King Amalric of Jerusalem was perhaps the most different out of all the previous kings due to the fact that he had his eyes fixed on the southwest. He wished to conquer the rich Egyptian territories instead of putting up a fight in the north, where Nur-ed Din was still a big problem. Maybe the reason behind his desire for Egypt was the ongoing political crisis of the Fatimids, as well as the friendly relations between the king and the Byzantine emperor, which gave him leeway to focus his attention on the south.

By the start of the 1160s, Egypt was deep into a period of turmoil and did not really have the power or resources to contest other major actors in the region, most notably Jerusalem. The power was not really in the hands of the Fatimid Caliph. Instead, the vizier, Shawar, was in control behind the scenes. However, Shawar was quickly ousted by another man by the name of Dirgham, who forced the former vizier to flee north to Syria. This struggle was quickly noted by both young King Amalric and Nur ad-Din, with both rulers wishing to take over the remnants of the once-great Fatimid Caliphate for themselves and solidify their position as the sole power in the Middle East.

Amalric was the first to strike. In September 1163, the king's forces marched on Egypt, demanding that the Egyptians continue paying the yearly tribute. At first, Amalric and his army were victorious when they confronted Dirgham's forces near Pelusium, forcing them to retreat to the city. However, when the Christians laid siege, the Egyptians decided to destroy the dams on the Nile River, flooding the lands and forcing Amalric to give up. Grand Master Bertrand, who had been released from captivity by then, accompanied his king with a group of Templars. He played a role in the negotiation between the two sides, with the Egyptians promising to continue paying tribute to Jerusalem.

In the meantime, Nur ad-Din was still unstoppable in the north. While Amalric was busy fighting with the Fatimids and making no real progress in capturing more territory, Nur ad-Din decided to attack Tripoli and weaken the Christian positions in the north. Here, however, the Templars proved their worth once again, scouting out the enemy's positions ahead of time and ambushing them at night. The Templars, who were fewer in numbers and led by Gilbert de Lacy, an experienced English warrior who had joined the order some years prior, quickly routed Nur ad-Din's army. They even forced the sultan to flee for his life barefoot from his camp. Although this encounter did delay Nur ad-Din for quite some time, an interesting development that followed his defeat would change the history of the Middle East forever.

After suffering a defeat against Gilbert de Lacy and the Templars, Nur ad-Din retreated and started building his forces back up to renew his assault on the Christian lands. It was then that the sultan received an unexpected visitor from the south: Shawar, the ousted vizier of Egypt, who had fled to Syria. Shawar approached Nur ad-Din with a proposal. He offered to march his armies down to Egypt and overthrow Dirgham. If they succeeded, Shawar promised to pay the sultan an annual tribute in return for his help. Nur ad-Din instantly liked the idea of attacking Egypt. In fact, he had been thinking about it himself for quite some time, since the start of the unstable period in the region. Instead of riding south himself, he sent Shirkuh, one of his trusted generals, with a sizeable force. In the meantime, he would focus on the Latin kingdoms in the north. An up-and-coming young man by the name of Salah ad-Din Yusuf ibn Ayyub would accompany Shirkuh in the Egyptian campaign and play a big role in the following events. He eventually became known as Saladin.

The Syrians saw great success against the Egyptians. Shirkuh confronted Dirgham's forces near Pelusium and defeated them with relative ease, killing their leader. Even though Shawar was back in power by the spring of 1164, thanks to the effort of Nur ad-Din's forces, he demanded that they quickly leave the Egyptian lands, declaring that they posed a potential threat to his kingdom. Shirkuh, however, had other plans in mind. He took the town of Bilbeis and fortified it, while Shawar sent an envoy to Jerusalem for help, promising the king, as well as his military order, huge sums of money and an array of gifts in return. King Amalric, realizing that he had the opportunity to wipe out a big chunk of Nur ad-Din's forces, assembled an army mainly comprised of Templars and marched south to lay siege to Shirkuh's position. The Syrians held out for more than three months in the fortified town, after which Amalric decided to break off the siege since Nur ad-Din had renewed the attack on the Christian factions in the north. The king of Jerusalem believed that the northern threat was more imminent and dangerous than helping Shawar in Egypt, so he turned back with his army to help defend against Nur ad-Din in the siege of Harenc (Harim) in Antioch.

Before Amalric was able to get to Antioch, a Christian alliance of Antioch, Tripoli, Armenia, and even the Byzantine Empire, led by Prince Bohemond III of Antioch, had assembled its troops to defend the region. It has to be noted that Bohemond had more than six hundred Templars with him, which made up the main punching power of his army. At first, the Christians forced the Muslims to retreat, but the Christians chased them forward, charging straight into an ambush and suffering a decisive defeat. All the leaders of the Christian forces, including Prince Bohemond, Count Raymond of Tripoli, and Byzantine General Constantine Coloman, were captured. It was a disaster and yet another victory for the Muslims against the Latin kingdoms. King Amalric could not help his fellow Christians in the north and was also unsuccessful against the Syrians in Egypt. He was only able to negotiate for Shirkuh to evacuate the territory immediately with the remainder of his forces.

A Change of Heart

Surprisingly, soon after these events, the relationship between the Templar Order and King Amalric of Jerusalem would start to worsen, according to William of Tyre, although he does not dive too deeply into the details. Apparently, Shirkuh continued to attack the Christian positions after his exit from Egypt. He assaulted two cave fortifications that were under the control of the Templars, who surrendered to the Muslim general without putting up a fight. In the meantime, Amalric had heard of Shirkuh's plan and tried to pursue him throughout Jordan to contest his move on the Templar positions. However, the king was late, as the news of the fall of the fortified territories reached him before he could catch up with the invaders. According to William of Tyre, twelve Templars who had fled from the site encountered the king and his small relief force. Amalric was infuriated with the Templars, claiming that they did not care about the kingdom's integrity and accused them of treachery. The king ordered the twelve Templars to be publicly hanged at the gallows and returned back to Jerusalem. This act, justifiable or not, caused the order and the king to frown upon each other, marking one of the most significant turns the relationship between the two parties had taken since the order's creation.

Because of this incident, the Templars would not join King Amalric in the future expeditions in Egypt, which lasted for the remainder of the 1160s. The king was really keen on taking over the

Egyptian lands, and he would continue his campaigns with or without the Templars' help. Still, perhaps the lowest point in his relationship with the order happened five years after the first development. This time, it was more complicated.

The Assassins—a secretive military Shi'a organization that had originated from Castle Alamut in Persia but had established a somewhat strong foothold in Outremer by the 1170s—were continuing to be a thorn in the side of the Sunni Muslims. They opposed the bloodthirsty nature of the jihad, which had been used by many rulers to justify their war effort against the Christians. With the rise of Nur ad-Din and the decline of Fatimid Egypt, the Assassins had correctly recognized that their position in northeastern Syria was under threat from the Sunnis.

The main headquarters of the Assassins was the fortress of Masyaf in the mountainous Jebel al-Sariya region. From there, they would conduct their secretive operations of assassinating powerful individuals who they thought were a threat to the organization and disturbed peace and stability in the region. For example, they murdered Count Raymond II of Tripoli because the count wanted to take their castle for himself. This policy of murdering tyrannical leaders was due to the Assassins' inability to field armies or squads, unlike the Templars, due to their relatively smaller size. By increasing their notoriety, however, the Assassins forged a rivalry with the Knights Templar, which held strong fortifications near the Shi'a organization and was constantly trying to limit its activity.

Starting from late 1153, the balance of power shifted in favor of the Templars, as they were granted more and more castles and continued to build up their possessions, forcing the Assassins to pay an annual amount of two thousand bezants (Byzantine gold coins). The murder of an Assassin envoy in the early 1170s would see the relationship between the Templar Order and the Assassins deteriorate completely, with the two officially becoming enemies.

This also worsened the already poor relationship between the Templars and King Amalric.

Sometime in 1173, an Assassin envoy was sent to King Amalric, according to William of Tyre. The messenger had been sent to Jerusalem to negotiate the terms of tribute to the Templars. According to William of Tyre, the Assassins were ready to convert to Christianity if the Templars agreed to exempt them from paying the tribute and not disturb their actions. The implications of this agreement were huge. In a way, it made sense for the Assassins to convert since they were the only party practicing Shi'a Islam in the region and were frowned upon by Nur ad-Din and the rest of the Sunni world. Also, their conversion would make their relations more favorable with the Latin kingdoms, with both sides using each other's experience and expertise in overcoming a common enemy.

William of Tyre suggests that their wish to convert to Christianity was propagated by the newly elected leader of the Assassins, whose name he does not mention in his account, although he calls him an "eloquent man of very sharp brain."[9] The new leader had collected different sacred writings of other religions and compared them to Islam. He came to the conclusion that the Shi'a ways of living were not optimal. He even encouraged his men to break basic Muslim traditions like drinking alcohol and eating pork.

So, when the envoy arrived at King Amalric's court, he was happily received, as the king saw the potential that lay in the agreement. To not upset the Templars, Amalric proposed that he would pay the two thousand bezants to the order from his own treasury as compensation. The talks went smoothly, and the messenger was set to return back to Castle Masyaf to finalize the agreement. He was to be accompanied by a member of the king's guard; however, he was murdered by the Templars just outside of Tripoli.

---

[9] Hill (2018), p. 76.

King Amalric had guaranteed the envoy's safety, granting him royal protection and respecting his status as a diplomat. This meant that the murder was a treacherous act, jeopardizing everything that had been agreed upon by the two parties. It was also seen as a shameful display, and the Assassins severed the agreement and refused to contact Jerusalem following the incident. But why exactly did the Templars do it? While the exact motive is not known, a chronicler named Walter Map writes about the greed of the Templars influencing this decision. He claims the Knights Templar, being a military organization and thriving on war, could not allow for the cessation of hostilities in the region. There was also the matter of greed, a common Templar motivator according to both Walter Map and William of Tyre. The two thousand bezants that had been paid by the Assassins every year was certainly nice for the order, and giving it up would have been very difficult, even if Amalric partially compensated what the Templars would have lost.

On the other hand, the Grand Master at the time, Odo of Saint-Amand, sent a letter to King Amalric, apologizing on behalf of his brother, who, as Odo claimed, was reckless in his actions and did not have approval. He promised the king that the Templar who had committed the crime, a knight by the name of Walter of Mesnil, would be sent to the pope to be tried, underlining the fact that the king had no authority over punishing the brother since the order only answered to the papacy. Later on, the Templars would claim that the Assassins did not deserve to be given the chance of conversion to Christianity and that they would contribute nothing to the defense of the Latin kingdoms. They supported this idea by saying that the secret organization had abandoned the idea of accepting the new religion once the news of their envoy reached them.

Whatever the case, the murder of the Assassin envoy was horrific, and it strained the relations between King Amalric and the Knights Templar even more.[10]

[10] Napier, G. (2011). *The Rise and Fall of the Knights Templar*. History Press. Chapter 4.

Hill, P. (2018). *The Knights Templar at War, 1120–1312*. Pen & Sword Military. Part 2.

Martin, S. (2011). *The Knights Templar*. Oldcastle Books. Chapter 2.

Nowell, C. E. (1947). "The Old Man of the Mountain." *Speculum*, 22(4), 497–519.

Chapter 7 – The Rise of Saladin

Saladin has become one of the most recognized names in military history. So far, we have only mentioned him as a young warrior who accompanied the Syrian general Shirkuh in Egypt. However, as time would show, Saladin would rise to become a powerful, feared, and well-respected man not only in the Middle East but also in Europe. In response to Saladin's rise, the Knights Templar would demonstrate the full might of the order. This chapter will cover how Saladin became a threat to the Templars and how the brothers struggled to overcome the challenge he posed to the Christian world.

Montgisard

King Amalric died in 1174, leaving the kingdom in the hands of his young leper son Baldwin IV. The teenage Baldwin was, as one would imagine, not competent enough in ruling when he was put in the position of king. In addition, his kingdom was in shambles, as the greedy Frankish lords had been squabbling over territories in the lands controlled by the Kingdom of Jerusalem. A similar situation was going on in Nur ad-Din's sultanate. The great sultan had died the same year as Amalric, making internal politics very complicated. Rival Muslim atabegs from Mosul, Aleppo, Cairo, and Damascus fought each other for superiority.

It was at this time that the young Saladin, an experienced general who had proven his worth in the Egyptian campaigns and against the Christians, managed to unify most of the rival atabegs under his rule, convincing them to join him and continue the jihad against the Christians instead of fighting between themselves. It is thought that he succeeded in doing this because of his reputation as a pious, god-fearing man. He was respected all throughout the Muslim world for his manners and ethics. These traits complemented his amazing fighting prowess, a skill for which he was known amongst the Franks. It must be said that, unlike the other Muslim leaders who had risen to prominence before him, such as Zengi and Nur ad-Din, Saladin was not as ruthless and bloodthirsty, especially when comparing his attitude toward the Christians. While he

Saladin

https://commons.wikimedia.org/w/index.php?curid=37860893

believed that they should be driven out of Outremer, he also understood why the Crusaders were motivated to fight. He thought their cause was just as noble as the Muslims. Thus, a new era of rival rulers was about to start in the East, with Saladin as the main leader of the Muslim world on one side and young Baldwin IV on the other, who was perhaps not as experienced as his counterpart but had the entourage and the support of the Templars and the other nobles of Outremer.

The first encounter between Saladin and the Christians would occur in 1177. For the first three years as the true sultan of the Muslim world, Saladin tried to unify his realms. He had taken Damascus and nearly succeeded in the siege of Aleppo but had to retreat. Still, he managed to unite the Muslims in most of Syria and established firm control over Egypt. Cairo was used as his main city. In 1177, his sultanate stretched from the Nile to Mesopotamia, which was an impressive feat that no Muslim ruler was able to achieve after the arrival of the Crusaders.

After the reunification of the Muslim lands, Saladin decided to turn his attention to the Christians and finish the process of driving them out of the Holy Land. Saladin's actions were closely monitored in the Latin kingdoms, and everyone realized the threat he would pose if he was able to launch an offensive with unified Syria and Egypt strengthening his back. So, when Saladin entered the lands controlled by the Christians in northern Sinai with a large army, King Baldwin IV was quick to answer. According to the accounts of William of Tyre, Saladin's army was huge, counting more than twenty-five thousand troops, most of which were experienced cavalry divisions. Saladin's entourage was the elite Mamluk contingent; the Mamluks were heavily armored shock cavalry from Egypt and were thought to be unstoppable on an open field.

It was logical that Saladin would attack either the city of Ascalon or the Castle of Gaza as his first target. King Baldwin, who had received intelligence of Saladin's moves, had fortified Ascalon, as he believed Gaza was in the safe hands of the Templars and could be quickly reinforced in case of a siege. The young king had anticipated correctly, for Saladin soon appeared at the doorstep of Ascalon. He chose to avoid a confrontation at Gaza, which was located closer to the Egyptian border. Baldwin sallied out with his forces, eager to meet Saladin in battle, but he was advised to retreat to the city since the opposing army was much larger than what he had expected.

The Muslims realized that they had effectively cornered the Christian army in Ascalon. They knew they would be relatively unopposed if they entered the heart of the kingdom, so they started to march toward the poorly defended Jerusalem and raided the lands along the way. King Baldwin realized the situation would be desperate if Saladin's army reached the Holy City, so he decided to chase after the enemy with a small force of his most elite troops, which would allow him to move quickly to catch up with Saladin. He sent to Gaza for help, assembling a small but very professional force of about four hundred mounted knights, plus eighty Templars led by Grand Master Odo of Saint-Amand. In addition, the king brought about two thousand infantrymen who would support his elite vanguard. The king planned to surprise the Muslim forces, which were slowly moving toward Jerusalem, from the north and disrupt their advance until more reinforcements showed up.

King Baldwin caught up with Saladin on November 25th, 1177. The Muslim army was crossing a narrow mountainous pass southeast of Ramla at Montgisard, causing them to stretch their numbers. Due to the disadvantage of the terrain, the Muslims' numerical superiority was ineffective. The Christians decided to act quickly and decisively, knowing that if the enemy managed to get out of the area, they would struggle in a head-to-head battle. Before their offensive, William of Tyre wrote that the Christian forces "arranged their lines according to military rules, disposing in proper order those who to make the first attack and the reserves who were to come to their aid."[11] This probably hints at the Templars' role of heading the organization of the troops and leading them into battle.

Then Baldwin's troops charged Saladin's northern flank headfirst without any hesitation, aiming to break through the front lines and get to the sultan himself. According to one chronicler, Ralph of Diss, the Templar contingent bonded together "as one man...turning neither left nor right...recognizing the battalion in which Saladin commanded many knights and manfully approached it."[12] The Templars slaughtered their way into the heart of Saladin's army, which was slow to mobilize against the surprise attack. Although Saladin managed to escape, leaving much of his equipment behind in order to run away faster with a small number of his Mamluk knights, most of the Muslim forces were chased down and slain.

It was a huge victory for the Christians; in fact, it was one of the most significant during the existence of the Crusader States. With it, King Baldwin narrowly managed to avoid the loss of Jerusalem and forced Saladin to retreat to Egypt. For days, the scattered Muslim soldiers would be cut down, with the Christian forces looting their corpses and taking the loot back to their king. All in all, the victory at Montgisard brought a sigh of relief to King Baldwin, as it gave him a chance to regroup and rethink his strategy against Saladin, who he knew would eventually return. The king had also, in effect, repaired the damaged relations between the crown and the Knights Templar. The Templars were praised for a long time after the battle because of their bravery and fighting at Montgisard, as they had been the ones who led the king's forces to victory. Still, despite this decisive victory, Baldwin IV had lost quite a few of his troops in the encounter, and while he had, for the time, driven Saladin out, the war was not over. The victory at Montgisard helped boost the

[11] Hill (2018), p. 81.

[12] Hill (2018), p. 81.

morale of the Christians, but the years that followed would prove to be difficult to endure, as a succession crisis and an array of internal problems destabilized the kingdom, giving Saladin a chance to retaliate.

Jerusalem's Succession Crisis

After the Battle of Montgisard, Saladin and Baldwin agreed to a truce, which was very much needed by both sides. For Saladin, it would give him more time to regroup after his defeat against the Christians and think of a new plan of action. For Baldwin, peace would relieve his kingdom from the constant pressure Saladin's sultanate exerted, giving him time to organize a better defense. However, a new Templar castle, Chastelet, located in a strategically important location near Jacob's Ford about ten miles southwest of Damascus, was taken by Saladin in violation of the agreement. The sultan claimed that Baldwin had agreed not to fortify the Jacob's Ford area since it was very close to the city of Damascus and posed a threat to the safety of the Muslims in Syria.

Chastelet was an impressive fortification located at the narrow crossing point of the ford. By early 1179, even though the Templars were not done building the castle, it had been constructed to the point where it could have been used defensively in case of an attack. All in all, the establishment of the Knights Templar in the area at Castle of Chastelet would have meant that caravans traveling from Egypt to Syria would have to go under the observation of the Christians, making the route unreliable. Saladin initially offered Baldwin 60,000 dinars to abandon the construction, an amount he later increased to 100,000 dinars. Still, Baldwin refused, making Saladin launch an offensive on Chastelet.

He arrived at the castle in May but was forced to retreat when one of his emirs was killed by Templar archers. In June, the Christians would mount an assault on Saladin, led by Templar Grand Master Odo and Raymond of Tripoli. This time, Saladin reigned supreme, defeating the Christians and capturing Odo of

Saint-Amand. It was the second time the Templar Grand Master had been a captive of a Syrian sultan, as he had been captured years earlier in 1156 with Bertrand de Blanchefort, who was the Grand Master of the order at the time. The two were quickly released from captivity thanks to the ransom paid by the Byzantine emperor. This time, however, Odo declined to be exchanged for a captured Muslim general, and he eventually died in prison in 1180.

Arnold of Torroja would replace him as the new Templar Grand Master. He had previously been the Master of the Templars in Spain and Provence. Arnold was an experienced man and quick to indulge himself in the administrative matters of the East, urging the Latin kingdoms to unite and face the threat of Saladin. His time as the Grand Master of the order was unfortunately cut short. In 1184, he decided to travel to Italy with Patriarch Heraclius and the Grand Master of the Knights Hospitaller, Roger des Moulins. They wanted to spread the word of Saladin's rise and ask for Western help.

Arnold could not deliver the message himself, however, as he died during the journey. He was replaced by Gerard de Ridefort, a charismatic person and the former marshal of Jerusalem, who would be remembered as arguably one of the worst Grand Masters at making big decisions. Around the same time, King Baldwin IV died of leprosy at the age of twenty-four. The years that followed would see the Grand Master and the Knights Templar as a whole becoming involved in the succession crisis of the Kingdom of Jerusalem.

The late leper king had no heir, so his ten-year-old nephew, Baldwin V, ascended to the throne under the patronage of Count Raymond of Tripoli. Unfortunately, the bad genes of the family showed once again, as young Baldwin soon fell ill and died, only lasting one year as the king of Jerusalem. Baldwin IV, however, had thought ahead. He had stated in his will that if his heir died at a young age, the rule of the Kingdom of Jerusalem would be entrusted to Count Raymond until a suitable new king could be found, preferably someone from Europe. Count Raymond, in fact, was already an experienced leader, so having him remain as regent after Baldwin V's death was a good idea, even more so because he managed to renegotiate a ceasefire agreement and a four-year non-aggression pact with Saladin.

Still, a power vacuum existed in the kingdom, with the Frankish nobles of Outremer soon recognizing that Raymond had not found a replacement by late 1186. In September of 1186, Baldwin IV's sister, Sybil, would claim that she was the legitimate heir to the throne, even though succession laws at the time excluded females. She revolted against Count Raymond and declared her husband, Guy of Lusignan, the new king. Interestingly, Grand Master Gerard was an avid supporter of this move, leading some historians to believe that Sybil and Guy had promised the Templars more power for their support.

Unsurprisingly, Guy of Lusignan was not exactly loved by his subjects. For one thing, he was seen as a usurper by the Frankish nobles, who believed that his claim to the throne of Jerusalem was weak. In addition, he was not really considered high nobility since he did not have an impressive background like the other possible choices. The only ones who sided with him, besides the Templar Grand Master, were power-hungry nobles, such as Reginald (Raynald) of Chatillon, who had a terrible reputation. Reginald was an unpredictable person, having been imprisoned by the Syrians for about sixteen years, which had probably caused his hatred toward the Muslims. After his release in 1176, he would set out on several anti-Muslim expeditions outside of Jerusalem-controlled territories and raided trade caravans that were trying to reach Syria from Egypt. In 1182, he had gone even further by raiding merchant ships in the Red Sea and Muslims who were traveling to the city of Mecca. Needless to say, the fact that King Guy had surrounded himself with people like Reginald of Chatillon and a rather rash Templar Grand Master was not a great sign.

The Fall of Jerusalem

It can be argued the recklessness of these two singlehandedly sabotaged any potential talks of peace with Saladin and angered the sultan beyond belief. First, in 1186, the peace between the Muslims and the Latin kingdoms, which had been finally agreed upon by Count Raymond, was jeopardized when Reginald attacked a Muslim merchant caravan. He killed the Egyptian entourage and looted their goods. Saladin was furious and turned to Count Raymond for an explanation. The count had nothing to do with Reginald's actions and told the sultan this.

Then, he brokered another peace agreement between his lands in Tripoli and his wife's domains in Galilee, giving Saladin his word that nothing like this would be repeated again in exchange for mercy for himself. Over the years, Count Raymond had grown pretty close to the Muslim ways of life and understood their customs fairly well. He had been a prisoner in Syria, but instead of hating the Muslims, he developed a respectful attitude toward them, which explains his relative success in the talks with Saladin. However, little did Count Raymond know that his efforts would once again be for nothing.

Soon after the incident, Raymond, on one side, and Guy and his entourage, on the other, decided to meet in the count's lands to talk about the ongoing situation in the Holy Land and settle on some sort of an agreement to improve their relations. They all realized that petty infighting would only speed up the doom of the Christians in the East. They agreed to meet at the town of Tiberias on the Sea of Galilee. The delegation, which included the Grand Masters of both the Templars and the Hospitallers, had marched out of Jerusalem and decided to stay at Templar Le Féve for the night. Before their arrival, however, Raymond had received word from Saladin's envoy to let some Muslim troops pass through his lands, a proposition he accepted because of his truce with the sultan. Unfortunately for the count, he was too slow to let the arriving delegation know about the Muslim troops.

The Templar squad under Grand Master Gerard, which counted only ninety brothers, as well as fifty more from the Hospitallers and secular knights, decided to attack. Their small force, however, was nothing in comparison to Saladin's seven-thousand men. Although Gerard decided to confront the Muslims on May 1st, 1187, at the Spring of Cresson, Grand Master Roger of the Hospitallers advised him not to proceed with the attack. The ensuing battle was a complete massacre, with the Muslims winning easily over the Christian knights. Grand Master Gerard managed to escape with two other knights while everyone else, including the Grand Master of the Hospitallers, was slain on the battlefield.

Saladin was not content with the victory at Cresson. His encounter with the Christians at Cresson was yet another instance of a broken peace agreement from the Latins. He was fed up with the untrustworthiness of the Franks and continued his march to Tiberias, besieging the city. Count Raymond realized that his treaty with Saladin was once again dead, and he had ridden out of the city before the arrival of the Muslim forces to meet with King Guy in Jerusalem and make up with him. By the end of June, King Guy had called for reinforcements from all over his realm and assembled a force of more than twelve thousand troops, which included large contingents from the Templars, Hospitallers, Turkish mercenaries, and infantrymen from the Frankish lords. By answering the call, the Templars and Hospitallers had summoned most of the brothers who were fit for fighting, leaving most of their fortifications relatively unattended. Saladin, on the other hand, had received even more reinforcements at Tiberias, with his numbers reaching about twenty thousand men. Tiberias would quickly fall to the sultan, and the countess of Tripoli would be trapped inside the castle.

It was looking desperate for the Franks, who, despite assembling an army, were hesitant to launch an offensive against the Mamluks. It was the middle of summer, and attacking in the extreme heat would put the Christians at a disadvantage. Plus, they correctly assumed that they would be outnumbered. Count Raymond advised King Guy to take a defensive position, even though his wife was a prisoner of the sultan and his lands were directly under threat from the Muslims. At first, the king listened. However, Grand Master Gerard thought otherwise. While the Christian army was encamped at Sephoria, he persuaded King Guy not to listen to the cowardly Count Raymond. The Grand Master told the king that losing Tiberias and allowing the Muslim force to move around and raid his lands freely was a shameful display. This was all Guy needed to hear. A day later, on July 3rd, 1187, he and his army rode out of Sephoria to meet Saladin at Tiberias.

The Christians decided to approach Saladin's position from the north through the hills of Galilee, arriving at the village of Lubya. They marched in the traditional column formation, with Count Raymond at the front, followed by the heart of the army with King Guy, and the Templar and Hospitaller contingents at the very back. Saladin had heard of the Christian offensive and sent out mounted archer divisions to harass the enemy and prolong their march. This had a devastating effect on the Christians, who would come under fire from the smaller Muslim squadrons again and again. They were never able to chase them down. Finally, the king received word from the Templars at the back, urging him to stop his advance. The king was forced to camp in the hilly region known as the Horns of Hattin.

Their situation was looking doomed. The Christians had no reliable water supply nearby. They were exhausted from the constant harassment and marching in the heat, and they were encamped in an uncomfortable position. Allegedly, Count Raymond realized what was going on and said aloud, "The war is over. We are dead men. The Kingdom is done for."[13] During the

[13] Martin, (2011), p. 69.

night, Saladin reached the Christians from the south. His men made a great fire, and in the morning, the breeze took the smoke over to the Christian camp in the north, making their lives even more difficult. As dawn broke on July 4th, Saladin's men attacked the Christians, splitting the army in half. King Guy's demoralized troops fought as hard as they could but were quickly overwhelmed by the might of Saladin's army. The Horns made it even more difficult for them to escape, as the Muslims overran their positions.

The Muslims claimed a decisive victory and slew most of the Franks. The Muslims walked away from the battle with an array of valuable prisoners, including Grand Master Gerard, King Guy, and Reginald of Chatillon. They also claimed an invaluable Christian relic for themselves, the True Cross, which had been transported from the Church of the Holy Sepulchre to boost the morale of the fighters and remind them of their cause of fighting for Jesus.

The Battle of Hattin was the final decisive blow. The prisoners were taken to Damascus, where the sultan spared the lives of the king and the Grand Master but publicly executed Reginald, who was hated. As for the captured Templars, he forced them to either convert to Islam or die. The Templars, to nobody's surprise, refused to give up Christianity, bravely offering themselves to be hanged or beheaded, believing they were dying as martyrs in the name of Jesus for a greater cause. This almost fanatical devotion of the Templars to their religion was one of the main reasons for Saladin's negative attitude toward the order. In Damascus, he executed more than two hundred Templars, only sparing their Grand Master.

Saladin then turned his attention to the now undefended lands of the Kingdom of Jerusalem. As we have already mentioned, the remaining Christian cities were left with no real garrisons since they had been sent to support the main army, which made it very easy for Saladin to take the Holy Land by storm. One by one, the cities and fortresses for which the Christians had sacrificed a lot, like

Ascalon, Gaza, and Acre, fell into the hands of the sultan without any opposition. He finally reached the most important city of them all—Jerusalem—in October of 1187 and marched into the city.

Even though Saladin was tolerant and respectful toward the Christian population of the town and allowed the Church of the Holy Sepulchre to continue existing as a Christian monastery, he forced the Templars to abandon the Al-Aqsa Mosque, the place where the order had been founded. In fact, no Templar would ever be able to set foot in the place of their origin ever again. However, the Christians were far from done when it came to fighting for the Holy Land.[14]

---

[14] Hill, P. (2018). *The Knights Templar at War, 1120–1312.* Pen & Sword Military. Part 2.

Martin, S. (2011). *The Knights Templar.* Oldcastle Books. Chapter 2.

Humphreys, R. S. (1977). *From Saladin to the Mongols: The Ayyubids of Damascus, 1193–1260.* SUNY Press. Chapter 1.

Chapter 8 – The Third Crusade

If it had been unclear before, the fall of Jerusalem signaled that the balance of power in the East had shifted heavily in favor of the Muslims. While the sultan had not completely wiped out the Christian presence in Outremer, he had substantially weakened it by taking key cities and fortresses in the Holy Land. The scattered Christians were in a panic, and just as they had done before when times were tough, they requested help from the West. This chapter will explore the response of the Christian world to the fall of Jerusalem in 1187 and take a closer look at the pivotal role the Knights Templar played in the effort to take back the lost lands.

The News Reaches Europe

By 1189, the only meaningful victory of the Christians versus Saladin had been the Battle of Montgisard. As we have already remarked, however, the victory at Montgisard only postponed the inevitable collapse of Jerusalem, which was struggling with internal problems while having to deal with the sultan at the same time. Despite the best efforts of the Templars, even their professionalism and military prowess were not enough to keep the Muslims at bay.

One of the biggest and, in a way, accidental problems with the Knights Templar as an institution was that there was no good way of replenishing the casualties the brothers suffered on the battlefield. While many people were willing to join the order, most of them were occupied with non-military matters, like running the numerous Templar holdings or financial affairs, while a minority of the Templars were knights who served in the armies. In addition, the fact that the Templars had embraced celibacy made it impossible for them to have children, which means they did not produce sons who could follow in their footsteps.

Over the years, due to the countless encounters with the Muslims, the Templars had exhausted their numbers, making it very easy for Saladin to overwhelm them in their own castles. Still, this did not diminish the role of the Templars; in fact, it made them even more valuable. Grand Master Gerard's influence in the succession crisis of Jerusalem describes the power the Templar Order held even when the situation in Outremer was dire. And even though Gerard could and should be criticized for the hasty and unwise decisions he took to exert his influence over King Guy, it could be argued that Jerusalem was doomed either way.

After the Battle of Hattin, Brother Terrence, the Templar Grand Commander, took charge of the order since Gerard had been taken as a prisoner by Saladin. Terrence was quick to realize that the remaining Christian forces were far from enough to put up a fight against Saladin. So, he wrote two letters and sent them to the pope and Count Philip of Flanders, who had recently visited the Holy Land. The Templar brother described the disastrous situation in the East and urged Europe to start a new Crusade. Pope Urban III, after receiving the letter in the spring of 1188 in Verona, reportedly had a heart attack due to the grave content of the letter and died on the spot. Gregory VII replaced Urban III, and although he only served as the new pope for no more than three months, he managed to circulate the letter among the European lords, spreading the news of the fall of Jerusalem around the continent. The pope urged the European kings to stop fighting each other and concentrate their attention and resources on a new expedition to the Holy Land. This would be the Third Crusade.

Interestingly, all of Europe suddenly swung into the Crusading spirit, much like the first time after the Council of Clermont. European lords from all over started to mobilize and answer the pope's call. Arguably, their motivation was not so much divine (they did not seek to remit their sins by fighting in the name of Christ). Instead, they wanted to prove themselves on the battlefield since the rival kings of Europe had not gained anything significant after years of warfare.

The Third Crusade presented a new opportunity. It could be a way to prove a ruler's worth not only to their subjects but also to the pope. Gaining more favor with the papacy could only prove to be advantageous. King William II of Sicily, for example, who was one of the first to receive the news, immediately sent a small fleet to Antioch to offer support and a potential escape mechanism for the Christians of the city. Eventually, England's King Richard I "the Lionheart," France's King Philip II, and Holy Roman Emperor Frederick Barbarossa would start the main campaign to the Holy Land.

The Kings' Crusade

The Kings' Crusade, as the effort would fittingly come to be known, would, much like the Second Crusade, be two separate journeys to the Holy Land. Emperor Frederick I of the Holy Roman Empire was the first to set out to Outremer, doing so sometime in early 1188. He had about twelve thousand men at his disposal. All the major German dukes, as well as his own son, followed the lead of the sixty-six-year-old emperor. Before the Germans started their march, however, the emperor sent envoys to the Hungarians, Byzantines, and Turks, asking them for military access, as his forces would have had to go through their lands. Frederick also sent an emissary to Sultan Saladin himself, as he had made a treaty with him earlier and thought it would have been only just to let him know of the end of the non-aggression pact.

The emperor's forces crossed Hungary without any losses, and they were welcomed by the locals, who let them pass peacefully. Anatolia would prove to be much more challenging for Emperor Frederick. Even though he had asked for military access, the Turkish mounted archers were problematic to deal with, just as they had been during the First and Second Crusades. Unlike his ancestor Conrad, Emperor Frederick was able to successfully repel the attack of the Turks, first at the Battle of Philomelion, where about two thousand Crusaders decisively defeated a ten-thousand-strong Turkish army, and then at the capital city of Iconium in May, sacking the city and killing about three thousand Turks in the process.

It all looked very promising for the German Crusaders, as they had approached the Latin kingdoms without having suffered any significant casualties. Unfortunately, the old emperor was not destined to take back the Holy Land. In June, Emperor Frederick Barbarossa's horse slipped while crossing the Saleph River, drowning the emperor. This heavily demoralized the German army, causing most men to return home to the pending election of the new Holy Roman emperor. Those who remained, about five thousand men in total, were led by Frederick's son, Frederick of Swabia, to Antioch, where they would eventually join up with the other Crusader army.

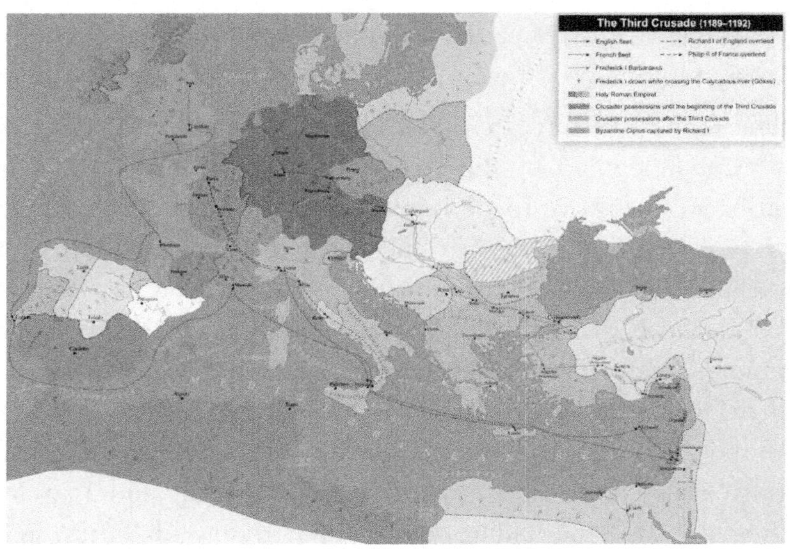

The route of the Third Crusade

The second and the main Crusader army was led by Richard I and Philip II. In fact, the two had stopped their war to unite for the Crusaders' cause and started mobilizing in January 1188. Their combined army was larger than Frederick's, counting upward of twenty thousand men, including a sizeable contingent of Templars led by their new Grand Master and a dear friend of Richard, Robert de Sable. The two kings agreed to muster their troops and meet at Sicily, from where they would set sail to the Holy Land. Unfortunately, Richard and Philip's relationship would suffer throughout the campaign, as the two kings would fall out over the issue of Richard's marriage. He had decided to break his betrothal with Philip's sister, Alys. For this reason, Philip left Sicily in March 1191 without waiting for the English to arrive. They would set out for Outremer a month later.

By the time King Richard arrived in the Holy Land, only Tripoli and Antioch were under firm Christian control. All the other possessions had been lost to Saladin. The Crusaders reunited at Acre in June, complete with the English and the French, as well as the remainder of the German troops (now under Leopold V of Austria since Frederick of Swabia had died) and an Armenian force under King Leo. Richard put himself in charge of the assault on the city. Taking Acre would be a significant achievement for the Christians if they wished to continue further military operations in the south. Acre fell a month later on July 12th. The Crusaders' inability to properly negotiate who should be put in charge of the city caused Richard to once again fall out with Philip and Leopold, who both decided to return to Europe with much of their forces. Still, this did not really affect King Richard. He had made it clear that he was capable of achieving more in the Holy Land.

After Acre, Richard took his men to Jaffa since taking the coastal city would make a potential assault on Jerusalem much easier. The Crusaders, however, were intercepted by the Muslim army in early September at Arsuf, which was about thirty miles away from the city. There, Saladin's men would suffer another decisive defeat by the Crusaders, who, despite being heavily outnumbered, managed to gain victory due to the tactical genius of Richard. The Templars also made up a significant portion of the army, so their efforts deserve recognition as well. Arsuf was Saladin's first major defeat after Montgisard, with Richard effectively taking control of the coastline and posing a serious threat to Jerusalem.

However, despite the successes at Acre and Arsuf, Richard and the Crusaders would never manage to take back the Holy City. Even though he had an open path to Jerusalem and came close enough to the city to see its walls, he decided to take the Templars' advice and not proceed any further. The order believed that even if the Crusaders managed to capture Jerusalem, it would be a near-impossible task to keep it, as it would require much effort and manpower. The Templars argued that most of the Crusaders would sail back to Europe instead of staying in Jerusalem, making it difficult to defend the Holy City. Richard listened to his advisors and chose to retreat to Ascalon. There, he rebuilt the city, which had been razed to the ground by Saladin, and chose to negotiate with the sultan instead, seeking to allow the free practice of Christianity to the pilgrims inside the city.

The king stayed at Ascalon for four months and then returned to Acre, only to hear the news that Saladin had taken Jaffa in just three days. In response, Richard decided to organize a counterattack and took the city back with the help of a small Templar force. After that, the negotiations with Saladin came to an end. The sultan recognized the Christian territories along the coast and agreed to a truce, while Richard agreed to dismantle the fortifications he had rebuilt in Ascalon. In early October 1192, Richard the Lionheart set sail to England, accompanied by a Templar entourage. He had achieved some progress during the Crusade.

The Aftermath of the Third Crusade

Before Richard left for England, he made sure to indulge himself in one more important matter—the succession of the Kingdom of Jerusalem. By the time the Crusaders reached the Holy Land, King Guy had been released by Saladin. Still, the nobility of Jerusalem was not exactly keen on his return, and when he tried to take power back, he was refused. Instead, the Frankish lords of Outremer favored Conrad de Montferrat, the German prince who had arrived in Outremer to support the Crusader States in 1188. Richard I endorsed Guy and wanted to install him as king. The matter would eventually be decided by a vote, with the Frankish nobility voting unanimously for Conrad. In theory, this made a lot of sense, judging by the fact that Conrad was of European descent and Guy's previous reign could not be characterized as successful.

Unfortunately, however, Conrad would be murdered by the Assassins just two days before he was to be crowned king. The barons of Jerusalem agreed to make King Richard's nephew, Henry of Champagne, the new king of Jerusalem. There still are doubts over whether Richard ordered the murder of Conrad, but nothing has ever been proven. As for Guy of Lusignan, Richard entrusted him with the control of the island of Cyprus, which he had actually conquered on his way to Outremer. In fact, in 1191, when Richard stopped at the island with his ships to resupply, he aided the people of Cyprus in getting rid of their Byzantine ruler, who was unpopular due to his positive relations with Saladin. After driving him out, Richard sold the island to the Templars for 100,000 bezants, who then sold it back to Richard and, therefore, Guy a year later. Choosing Guy as the leader of Cyprus meant that he was officially out of contention for the throne of Jerusalem. The island was a much more suitable place for him to rule since it was not nearly as strong or important as other Christian holdings in the East.

With the Third Crusade, the Christians managed to reclaim some of the lost territories in the Holy Land. Most importantly, they had now regained control of the coastline, making it more accessible for pilgrims and potential reinforcements to arrive from the West. In addition, they had significantly weakened Saladin's position, and the sultan would pass away soon after the end of the Third Crusade.

All in all, this Crusade was not nearly as unsuccessful as the second one. It can be argued that, in a way, the Crusaders were unlucky. Who knows what would have happened if Emperor Frederick Barbarossa had made it to the Holy Land with most of his army. Still, despite the infighting amongst the leaders of the Crusade and the relative lack of resources they had to work with, they achieved quite a lot, more than one would expect. Even though they did not capture Jerusalem, the Crusaders were probably right not to try an assault on the city, as it would result in more casualties and would be difficult to hold once the majority of the army returned home.

As for the Templars, just like the rest of the Christians of the East, they were given some breathing room after their struggles with Saladin. The new Grand Master, Robert de Sable, had proven to be a much more competent leader than Gerard, who was eventually beheaded by Saladin in 1189. After the Third Crusade, the Templars took their time to rebuild and regain their strength. They moved their headquarters to Acre and quickly started fortifying it, transforming it into the wealthiest and most important Christian city of the East. The brothers also contributed to the reconstruction of the destroyed castles that had been in their possession.

Most importantly, the Templars tried to regain the lost fortresses in the Amanus March, like Castle Gaston, which had been abandoned by the Muslims after being conquered in the 1180s. The Templars fought over Gaston with Leo of Armenia for more than two decades until, finally, the king decided to turn it and other Templar holdings over after being excommunicated by the pope.

Templar involvement in the Third Crusade was just as, if not more, prevalent than during the Second Crusade. The Templars were the driving force of King Richard's army, and they helped the king navigate the Holy Land. Grand Master Robert had played a similar role to Everard des Barres, advising and guiding the leader of the Crusade and striving for discipline and excellence in his army.

One very important development that followed the Third Crusade was the establishment of the Teutonic Order—one of the three major Christian military orders in history, alongside the Templars and the Hospitallers. Out of the three, the Hospitallers were the oldest, founded in 1070, some fifty years before the Knights Templar.

The Hospitallers' original purpose was not fighting. Founded by a group of merchants from Amalfi, the Hospital, as the name suggests, served as a place for the traveling pilgrims in the Holy Land to stay and be treated. The Hospital had close ties with the Church of the Holy Sepulchre, providing the pilgrims with any sort of humanitarian aid they might need. The order was highly popular from the very beginning and began receiving lands all over Outremer after the success of the First Crusade. In fact, it was officially recognized by the pope in the early 1110s, with Saint John the Baptist as their patron saint. After the election of their second Grand Master, Raymond du Puy, the Hospitallers adopted a military aspect as part of their lifestyle. This development coincided with the formation and rise of the Templars, which was a Christian military organization at the very beginning.

It is thought that the Templars would often guard the holdings of the Hospitallers in the early years since the Hospitallers had not yet incorporated militarism. However, under Grand Master Raymond, the organization came up with a new name: "the Order of the Knights of the Hospital of Saint John of Jerusalem." This name was inspired by their Templar counterparts, and the two became more and more alike. Just like the Templars, the Hospitallers would also make a name for themselves, and while their possessions and overall wealth and power were not as excessive as the Knights Templar, they were deeply trusted by the kings of Jerusalem and even rose to prominence in Europe. In fact, the order would continue its operations long after the dissolution of the Knights Templar, a matter we shall discuss further down the line.

As noted previously, the foundations laid by the Templars and the Hospitallers led to the creation of another very important Christian military order: the Order of the Teutonic Knights. The Teutons would be formed by those German Crusaders who chose to stay in the Holy Land after the Third Crusade (as you might recall, a large number of the German troops chose to return home after the death of their emperor). Those German knights who decided to stay joined a field hospital set up by a group of German pilgrims and merchants from Lubeck and Bremen. The headquarters were not nearly as impressive as those of the Templars and the Hospitallers. It was a tent made from sails located in the city of Acre. The Hospitallers had chosen Saint Mary as their patron, and when the German knights joined, they were named the Teutonic Knights of Saint Mary's Hospital of Jerusalem.

The Teutonic Order would officially be recognized by the Templars in 1198 at the Temple of Acre, incorporating it into the Christian Church. Over time, the Teutonic Knights would shift their base of operations from the Holy Land to northern and eastern Europe, becoming heavily involved in the politics of the Holy Roman Empire, Lithuania, Hungary, and other major European states. In fact, at the height of their power, they would establish their own state off the coast of the Baltic Sea and become a major actor in Europe.[15]

---

[15] Brand, C. M. (1962). "The Byzantines and Saladin, 1185–1192: Opponents of the Third Crusade." *Speculum*, 37 (2), 167–181.

Martin, S. (2011). *The Knights Templar.* Oldcastle Books. Chapter 2.

Hill, P. (2018). *The Knights Templar at War, 1120–1312.* Pen & Sword Military. Part 2.

Lotan, S. (2015). "The Teutonic Knights and their Attitude about Muslims: Saracens in the Latin Kingdom of Jerusalem and in the Baltic Region." *Fear and Loathing in the North: Jews and Muslims in Medieval Scandinavia and the Baltic Region*, 313-328.

Willoughby, J. (2012). "A Templar Chronicle of the Third Crusade: Origin and Transmission." *Medium Ævum, 81*(1), 126–134.

Part Three – The Fall of the Knights Templar

Chapter 9 – The Final Days in the East

Overall, even though the Christians managed to consolidate some of the lost territories thanks to the efforts of the Templars and King Richard in the Third Crusade, many questions still needed to be answered. Most importantly, how long would the "peace" between the Latin kingdoms and the Muslim world continue? In addition, there was also the issue of Jerusalem, as the Holy City was not under the control of the Christians.

As for the Templars, even though the order would manage to reclaim much of its strength, it was no surprise that it would not reach the level it had before. While the Knights Templar continued to build up their resources, expanding in Europe and reinforcing the frontlines in the East, the order would start declining in the decades following the recapture of Acre. This chapter will explore how the order was confronted with different challenges throughout the 13th century, starting an almost one-hundred-year period of instability and chaos that would eventually see the end of the Knights Templar.

The Fifth Crusade

The world was split over whether or not the Third Crusade had been a success. It has to be said that King Richard had made significant improvements for the Christians in the Holy Land. Perhaps if he had had the backing of the full Crusader force, he might have even gained even more than he did. As it stood, after Richard's departure from Outremer, Jerusalem was still in Saladin's hands. This was perceived as a viable reason for a new Crusade by Pope Innocent, whose efforts eventually resulted in the shameful events of the Fourth Crusade. Instead of arriving in the Holy Land, the Europeans sacked the city of Constantinople, which at that time was still under the Byzantine Empire's control.

Due to this, the Templar involvement in the Fourth Crusade was basically nonexistent. After all, the main purpose of the order was to fight against the Muslims and protect the interests of the Christian world. Warring with their Greek Orthodox Christian brothers did not fall on the Templar agenda. However, not long after the Fourth Crusade, in 1216, Pope Honorius III would finally make Pope Innocent's dream come true.

By then, Guillaume (William) de Chartres was the Grand Master of the Templars. The heavy Templar involvement in the Fifth Crusade was due to a letter he received from the pope, in which he was asked to meet with the leaders of the new Crusade to discuss the plan and oversee the operations. The same letter was received by the Hospitaller Grand Master, Guérin de Montaigu. Together, the two Grand Masters met with King Andrew of Hungary and Duke Leopold of Austria on the island of Cyprus. The funding of the expedition was also overseen by the Templars, as the money would be collected at the Paris Temple by Brother Haimard, the Templar treasurer, and be transported and accompanied by the knights of the order.

After much consideration, the Crusaders decided to launch an assault on the city of Damietta – a key Egyptian city located in the

Nile Delta. Surprisingly, after some initial struggles the Crusaders experienced during landing, Damietta was easily captured in mid-1218. By then, John of Brienne, King of Jerusalem, and Hugh I of Cyprus had also joined up with the rest of the forces. The Crusaders would be impressed by the skill of the Templars, especially given the fact that they were fighting in difficult conditions. Navigating the swamps and marshes of the Nile Delta was not easy, but the Templars were able to maneuver effectively both on horseback and on foot in difficult terrain. Their bravery was remarked upon by Oliver of Paderborn, who accounts much of the Crusaders' success to the Templars.

Unfortunately for the Templars, Guillaume de Chartres would die during the siege in late August. He was replaced by Peter de Montaigu—the brother of Guérin de Montaigu, the Grand Master of the Hospitallers. In an extraordinary circumstance in the history of these military orders, the same family was in charge of both the Templars and the Hospitallers.

The loss of Damietta prompted the Egyptian Sultan al-Kamil to send an interesting offer to the Crusaders in the autumn of 1219. In the letter, he offered to give Jerusalem and the True Cross back to the Christians in exchange for the recently captured Damietta. Perhaps the sultan thought that the establishment of a Crusader holding so close to the heart of his sultanate posed a serious threat. However, the Crusaders declined the offer for the same reason King Richard had done so decades earlier; they knew holding onto Jerusalem would take a lot of resources that Outremer still did not have.

In true Crusader fashion, the victory at Damietta would be followed by internal quarrels over who should be put in charge of the city, causing many of the men to hop on ships and abandon the Crusade. In addition, the Templars had their own problems in the north, as their Atlit Castle was under siege by the Muslims, who maintained the siege until November of 1220. For this reason, Peter de Montaigu had to send a number of his men northward, taking much of the strength and wisdom away from the Crusader army.

At that point, Cardinal Pelagius, the de-facto leader of the Crusade who had been sent from Rome by the pope himself, was considering a new assault on Cairo, the capital of the Egyptians. However, the two Grand Masters would argue that stretching the Crusader resources from Damietta to Cairo would be challenging, as they were not aware of the potential strength of the Egyptians. In fact, when the sultan realized that an attack on Cairo was imminent, he offered the Christians a ceasefire for a second time, now guaranteeing them a thirty-year truce and control over the city of Jerusalem and the lands that acted as a buffer between the Holy City and Egypt.

However, even though this offer seemed logical to accept, and Pelagius had been ordered by the pope to discuss any peace agreements, the cardinal denied the offer and set his eyes on Cairo. He did not listen to the advice of the Templar and Hospitaller Grand Masters. Cardinal Pelagius was banking on German reinforcements led by the newly elected Emperor Frederick II, the grandson of Frederick Barbarossa. Unfortunately for Pelagius, the Germans were nowhere to be seen, and he had already committed to an offensive on Cairo. This caused the Christians to overextend and be cut down by the Egyptian hit-and-run forces. This defeat eventually caused the cardinal to give up, forcing him to surrender Damietta back to the Egyptians. The Fifth Crusade was over.

Frederick II

Some Crusaders blamed the failure of the Fifth Crusade on Emperor Frederick II's absence. He had vowed to join the Crusade in 1212 at his coronation. Still, Frederick II was a very interesting figure who would come to define most of the future matters of Outremer. From an early age, Frederick II had an interest in studying the East and was fascinated with Arab culture. So much so, in fact, that he ruled as close to the Arabs as possible, residing in

Sicily (which was, at the time, a part of the Holy Roman Empire). His personal bodyguard was composed entirely of local Muslim Saracens. His curious nature and obsession with finding a connection between science and God also led to many believing the young emperor was an atheist. He would indulge himself in unruly experiments, as he would try to observe a man's soul leaving his body or how the organs of a dead man may have been affected by the evil or good things he had done in his lifetime. In short, Frederick II was not an ordinary ruler, and his motivations for taking up the cross and joining the Crusade were certainly different from his predecessors. It is clear he was not motivated by recapturing Jerusalem and did not believe the Muslims were his enemies.

His difficult character had, in fact, caused his delay in joining the Fifth Crusade. Pope Gregory had waited for him to journey to the Holy Land for a long time and, seeing that the emperor was stalling, excommunicated him. In a weird decision, Frederick took up the cross after being excommunicated, prompting the pope to excommunicate him a second time, even though he still had not recovered from his previous excommunication. Thus, it is not surprising to understand why not everybody in Outremer was exactly keen on the appearance of the double-excommunicated, weird, and potentially atheist Emperor Frederick when he finally landed at Acre in September of 1228. The news had already reached the Holy Land, and not everyone was looking forward to collaborating with the emperor.

This caused a big division in the ranks of the Christians, with most of the Frankish lords of Jerusalem, the Hospitallers, and the Templars all choosing to side with the pope's decision and not support Emperor Frederick. On the other hand, the Teutonic Knights were willing to help Frederick in his upcoming military endeavors due to their German ties. An important detail to understand is that Frederick's decision to come to Outremer was also because he had a legitimate claim to the throne of Jerusalem through his wife Isabella, who was the only child of King John de Brienne of Jerusalem. However, Isabella had recently passed away during childbirth, making Frederick a regent for his newborn son Conrad, who was next in line for Jerusalem's throne.

Soon after the arrival of Frederick, the Templars found themselves in a quarrel with the Holy Roman emperor. The emperor demanded loyalty from the Templars when he showed up with his forces at the Templar Atlit Castle. The Templars denied forfeiting the castle to the emperor but agreed, somewhat reluctantly, to join his Crusade. But to distance themselves, they stated they would only accompany Frederick because of their own goodwill and eagerness to reclaim the Holy Land. They also marched about a day's distance behind the emperor. The Hospitallers did the same. Surprisingly, even though Frederick's army was not large, only counting a couple of thousand men at best, his first move to Jaffa was very successful. Through diplomacy, Frederick managed to negotiate the control of Jerusalem.

With Jerusalem secured, Frederick had definitely made a statement to those who opposed him in Outremer, including the military orders, the patriarch, and the majority of the Frankish nobility. However, it can be argued that recapturing the Holy City was not a significant improvement for the Christian positions. Frederick had only managed to cede control of the actual city itself, not the lands surrounding it. This was important as, effectively, Jerusalem was on the southern border with Egypt, with no real buffer separating it from the Muslims, leaving it an easy target for potential invaders. In addition, the city was still isolated from the rest of the Holy Land; there was only a tiny, narrow corridor to the coastal cities, which could be easily exploited to cut off supply lines. Moreover, the whole agreement had been achieved due to the internal fighting of the Egyptians, who had no real time or resources to spend on defending Jerusalem from a potential Christian attack.

In fact, the talks about the control of Jerusalem are thought to have been started way before Frederick arrived in Outremer, as he had received an envoy from Sultan al-Kamil, who first proposed ceding the city in exchange for Frederick's help against Damascus. However, the two sides had not come to terms, but they laid down a basis for the talks that took place at Jaffa. And even though the alliance between Frederick and the Muslims against Damascus was not part of the deal, Frederick let the Muslims retain control of the Al-Aqsa Mosque. He allowed the practice of Islam in the city and banned the Templars from entering their historical headquarters.

Overall, it was still a victory for Frederick, despite the fact that he over-glorified his achievement. But what he did next was an even more politically motivated move to show his superiority over his opposition. On March 17th, 1229, after taking control of Jerusalem, Emperor Frederick entered the Church of the Holy Sepulchre and crowned himself the king of Jerusalem, a title that most of the Holy Land thought he had no right to. What makes this move even more ridiculous is the fact that Gerold of Lausanne, Patriarch of Jerusalem, who had been one of the fiercest critics of the emperor thus far, had ordered all the members of the church from practicing their religion as long as Frederick was in the city. This meant that there was no one in the Holy Sepulchre to crown Frederick, causing him to put the crown upon his own head. He literally crowned himself. Then, in the presence of the loyal Teutonic Knights who had accompanied the emperor, the new king of Jerusalem announced that he forgave the pope for excommunicating him and declared himself "God's Vicar on Earth," a title only held by the pope before.

The vast majority of the Christian world, both in the East and the West, was appalled by Frederick's actions. He had made a lot of powerful enemies in the Holy Land, including the Templars and the Hospitallers, who refused to follow the emperor any longer and returned to Acre, where the anti-Frederick sentiment was the strongest. The city was reportedly outraged by the emperor's actions. No one supported his claim, with most of the people believing that the rightful heir to the throne was Conrad, Frederick's son, who had still not come of age. Even as the father to the king, he was despised for his arrogance.

The relations between the Templars and the Crown of Jerusalem, an institution that was historically one of the closest allies of the order, deteriorated, reaching an all-time low because of Frederick's illegitimacy. It got so bad that there were eventually rumors going around that the brothers (the Grand Masters of the Templars and Hospitallers) wanted to assassinate the emperor and place somebody else on the throne. When Frederick arrived at Acre with his force, demanding those inside to surrender the city and declare their loyalty to their new king, he was swiftly denied by Grand Master Peter. The stand-off between the two sides continued for more than a month, with Frederick surrounding Acre and the Templar Atlit Castle with his forces, ordering them to shoot anyone who tried to enter or leave, especially the Templars.

Eventually, however, in late April 1229, Frederick learned of his lands in Europe being besieged by none other than John of Brienne, the former king of Jerusalem, who was now leading a papal army to punish Frederick's actions. (John had been pushed aside by Frederick after Frederick married John's daughter.) This news shocked Frederick and forced him to quickly return to Italy, abandoning Acre in early May. When the emperor left, the crowd threw rotten meat at him, once again demonstrating their hatred toward the self-proclaimed king. Still, Frederick's departure was not the end of his involvement in the East, as the Holy Roman emperor first left two of his trustees in the Holy Land and later sent Richard Filangieri, an imperial marshal, with a sizeable force to oversee his affairs. Filangieri and the rest of the supporters would settle in Tyre in 1231, while the rest of Outremer continued to oppose the emperor and refused to recognize him.

After Frederick's return to Italy, he continued posing a problem for the Templars, confiscating many of their possessions and refusing to hand them over, even after being ordered to do so by the pope, causing him to be excommunicated once again. The effects of Frederick's peculiar endeavors would be felt by the Templars and the rest of the East in the years to come, as outside involvement from the West had once again left the Holy Land destabilized and weakened.

The Conflict between the Orders

Despite the ongoing dispute about the succession of the Kingdom of Jerusalem, by some miracle, the Christians were still holding onto their lands. The truce that had been agreed upon by Frederick and al-Kamil would last for ten years until 1239, giving the Christians of the East a small window to build up their forces for a potential assault on their positions. Instead of that, however, as they had done before on many occasions, they could not come to terms with each other. Rival camps continued coexisting throughout the 1230s, with Richard Filangieri and the imperial supporters on one side and the Templars, Hospitallers, the patriarch, and the Franks on the other.

While it is true that during this period, some effort was made to weaken the Muslims, mostly through the combined efforts of the military orders, nothing significant was achieved. The Templars and the Hospitallers suffered several defeats, first at Hama and then at Atlit. It was becoming clear that the Latin kingdoms were losing their grasp on the Holy Land quicker than ever. In 1239, Pope Gregory urged the leaders of Europe to unite once again for a new Crusade, but no major powerhouse was interested in sending the resources necessary to conduct an expedition. As they most likely realized, due to past examples, it was doomed to achieve little anyway.

The only noble that answered the call was Theobald, King of Navarre and Count of Champagne, who arrived at Acre in

September of 1239 with a laughable force of no more than a thousand men. Still, any amount of help was welcome for the struggling Christians of the region, who, just like in the old days, immediately started drawing up plans for what was next. Theobald had incorrectly assumed the complexity of the politics of the East. Upon his arrival, he was convinced to launch an offensive in the south on Gaza and Ascalon. This decision was heavily influenced by the Templars, who had managed to negotiate a deal with Damascus by offering help in the war against the Egyptians (who held Gaza and Ascalon) in exchange for the Damascenes ceding control of the Templar castles that had been conquered by Saladin decades earlier.

However, before Theobald was able to muster up enough men to form a competent force, Count Henry of Bar decided to take matters into his own hands. He embarked on a secret expedition to Gaza with about 1,500 men of his own. Henry had not told any major baron of Outremer of this endeavor, hoping to capture Gaza by himself, which he incorrectly thought to be poorly defended. He did ask the Templars and Hospitallers for reinforcements, but this request was instantly rejected by the military orders. They knew this sort of an attack was foolish.

The orders were proven to be right when Henry's much smaller force was ambushed deep into Egyptian territory. The Muslims slew the Crusaders, killing Henry in the process and capturing more than six hundred men. It was a disaster for the Christians, whose chances of solidifying their positions were further reduced by Henry's reckless actions. However, surprisingly, the blame fell on the Templars and the Hospitallers, who were accused of treachery because they did not help the count in his campaign. This detail is thought to have been an incinerating factor for the increasingly poor relations between the West and the Templars, with the Templars being blamed for acting solely according to their own interests instead of doing what was right for the greater good.

The Western Christians, who would later put the Templars on trial for this and many other reasons (a topic that will be covered in the following chapters), did not understand why the order would deny an opportunity to fight against the Muslims—the people the Templars had sworn to fight in the name of Christ. The truth of the matter was that the military orders correctly recognized the unwise plan of attacking Gaza and saved themselves from an impending defeat. But the fact that they would involve themselves in the politics of the East on such a deep level, choosing sides and even dealing with the Muslims for their own benefit, created a level of suspicion surrounding the purpose of their existence—a suspicion that would be exploited in the coming decades.

The Templars would face even more complicated matters after the arrival of Richard of Cornwall, brother of King Henry III of England and the brother-in-law of Emperor Frederick II. Richard landed in the Holy Land in the autumn of 1240, and he immediately started a series of negotiations with the Muslims, as well as with the nobility of the East. The aim of his visit was to check Frederick's claims of the East; after all, the emperor was still the "king" of Jerusalem, but he had been away from his kingdom for a long time. The Englishman found the military orders, for the first time in a while, split regarding what was best for the good of the Holy Land, with the Hospitallers preferring a more diplomatic approach with the Egyptians in light of the Templars' decision to ally with the Damascenes to reclaim their long-lost castles. In fact, Richard was able to successfully negotiate the southern lands of Belvoir and Tiberias, as well as the release of the previously captured Christians at Gaza with the Egyptians, thanks to an earlier agreement the sultan had approved with the Knights Hospitaller. With this, even though some southern cities like Gaza, Nablus, and Hebron still stayed under Muslim control, Richard took charge of the surrounding territories, establishing the long-deserved buffer near the Holy City.

The brother-in-law of Frederick II was certainly content with himself when he set sail for England a year later in 1241, as he had reclaimed a sizeable landmass for the Christians while also undermining the Templars' influence in the region (remember, the order and the emperor hated each other). By siding with the Hospitallers, Richard had effectively swayed them more to the imperial side, forging a rivalry between them and the anti-Frederick Templars.

Still, the Templars did not sit back and watch Richard and the Hospitallers gain more influence. Templar Grand Master Armand of Perigord did not want to give up his order's alliance with the Damascenes, who had promised him the return of the old castles in the north. So, after the departure of Richard, a Templar force attacked the Egyptian town of Hebron and then successfully proceeded onto Nablus, achieving victory and sacking the city.

There was no denying that a wedge had been driven deep between the Knights Templar and the Knights Hospitaller, with both orders becoming each other's rivals in the following years. Both of them would be involved in the succession struggle of Jerusalem once again. This happened not long after the sacking of Nablus, after the arrival of Thomas of Aquino, who was supposed to accept the throne of Jerusalem in place of Prince Conrad, the son of Frederick II, who had finally come of age to become king. The Templars, however, perceived Thomas's arrival as the final step to their loss in the East. They thought that if he were to convince the Franks of Outremer to accept him as king, the order would lose much of its prominence to both the imperialist camp and the Hospitallers.

Thus, the Templars proceeded to do everything in their power to reduce Conrad's influence, claiming that Dowager Queen of Cyprus, Alice, was the person to whom the throne of Jerusalem really belonged. Then, in the summer of 1243, they were able to drive Conrad's supporters out of the Holy Land with some help from Italian merchants, who had their own unsettled grudges against the emperor. The Templars had triumphed over their long-time enemy. Despite their success, however, Grand Master Armand's concerns would eventually come true, as the whole of Eastern Christendom was not ready to fend off a new Muslim invasion that awaited them in the following decades.

The Battle of La Forbie

Decades of instability and internal struggles had greatly affected the Latin kingdoms. Two of their biggest competitors in the East—Cairo and Damascus—went to war in 1244. For the Latins, the situation was looking dire, as Egypt had made a close alliance with the Khwarazmians (Khwarezmians), a Sunni Turkish people who were fierce and brutal warriors. The Templars had allied themselves with the Damascenes, but even they knew that stopping Egypt would be very difficult once the Khwarazmians reinforced them. So, waiting for an inevitable offensive on their positions, the Templars, now with the help of the Hospitallers and the Teutons, with whom they had somewhat repaired their relations due to the impending threat, started building up fortifications in the major Christian cities of the East.

The Khwarazmians proved to be even more ruthless than they had anticipated. On their way to Egypt, they ran over every attempt of resistance by the Damascenes, destroying every villa and town on their way, including Tiberias and Nablus. In June 1244, about ten thousand of them had reached Jerusalem, which was thought to be their final stop before reaching Cairo and joining their forces with Egypt. The invaders laid siege on Jerusalem, which, to no one's surprise, was not able to hold. After a month, the city had fallen, and the defenses prepared by the military orders were not enough. The Khwarazmians stormed the city, massacring the local Christian population as they attempted to flee to Jaffa. The invaders then proceeded to violate the remains of the previous kings of Jerusalem at the Holy Sepulchre and set the city ablaze, only then deciding to continue their march to Egypt.

The Christians of Outremer were shocked by the news. A decision was taken to assemble what forces they could to meet the Khwarazmians before they reached their reinforcements. At Acre, the Franks called for their own reinforcements from Damascus, who arrived under the Damascene leader al-Nasir. The Templars, Hospitallers, and the Teutons assembled a combined force of about one thousand knights from all of the orders, which acted as the elite part of the Christian army. About six hundred secular knights were also present under Walter, Count of Jaffa, and Philip de Montfort of Tyre. Several other important figures of the East were also there, with the full army counting about ten thousand troops in total—the largest force the Christians had assembled since Hattin. In October, the Christians started their march south, hoping to catch the Khwarazmian army near Gaza and confront them in battle.

On October 17th, 1244, the combined army of the Christian nobility, the military orders, and the Damascene allies met the Khwarazmians in battle a couple of miles northeast of Gaza at the village of La Forbie. Unfortunately for the allies, the enemy had managed to meet up with the Egyptians, so their numbers were higher than what the Christians had expected. The battle, which lasted for two days, saw both sides fighting fiercely against each other. For the Latins, it was their final stand, as they had committed most of their capable men into the army. For the Egyptians and the Khwarazmians, it was a chance to break the Christians and overwhelm them in later encounters.

The first day ended with no major improvements for either side. The Templars, Hospitallers, and Teutons ensured high morale and discipline for the Christian infantry and were able to repel the enemy's cavalry charges. However, on the second day, the Damascene flank was hit, with the Egyptians and Khwarazmians managing to quickly break the Muslim allies of the Latins, forcing them to run for their lives. This, in turn, caused the Christian flank to become exposed, with the enemies taking swift advantage and running them down, killing as many men as they could.

The Christian army was almost fully destroyed. No more than fifty Templar and Hospitaller knights managed to escape from La Forbie. Grand Master Armand of Perigord, along with the count of Jaffa and several other important Latin figures, were captured, never to be seen again. La Forbie had shattered the dreams of the reunification of the Holy Land, as the Latin kingdoms would never be able to recover from their biggest loss since the Battle of Hattin.

After the battle, the supporters of Conrad and the imperialist camp put the blame on the Templars, claiming that the Damascenes' retreat was their fault since it had been the Templars' decision to ally with them in the first place. And while the order had played a crucial role in keeping Outremer together for so many years, there was no time for any failure, especially at this hour. Still, despite their criticism, the new Grand Master, Guillaume of Sonnac, who was elected three years later in 1247, probably because the order was unsuccessfully negotiating the release of Armand, continued to build up Templar holdings and ensure that a disaster like La Forbie never occurred again. Little did he know, much tougher times still lay ahead for the Knights Templar.

The Fall of Acre

Suffering another major defeat at La Forbie naturally prompted the West to answer with another Crusade. However, as was the case before, no one was really keen on venturing out to the Holy Land, as they did not believe their efforts would save the Latin kingdoms from falling. To make matters worse, Damascus fell to the Egyptians soon after their victory at La Forbie, meaning that the more unified Muslims now posed a bigger threat to the Christian positions than before. In addition, the succession crisis of Jerusalem and the internal fighting that came with it had not only deprived the Latin kingdoms of valuable manpower and experienced leaders but also made it even more difficult to find a potential reason for reunification, as different actors acted on their own personal interests and did not prioritize the greater good of the Christian East.

It did not look good for the Templars and the rest of the military orders that had been fighting for years to protect the Holy Land from their enemies. As we have already mentioned, it was becoming more and more difficult for them to replace their ranks, and they had lost much of their prized possessions throughout the 13th century. The Templars did not hold as many castles in strategic locations as they once did, and of those that they did control, few were garrisoned sufficiently enough to hold off a potential invasion. It was looking doomed for the Latin kingdoms.

Only King Louis IX of France answered the call for what would be known as the Seventh Crusade. Louis was a famously pious man and had vowed to venture out to the Holy Land once he recovered from his illness. In the end, the king arrived at Cyprus in September of 1248, where he was met by the new Templar Grand Master, Guillaume de Sonnac, and King Henry of Cyprus. The parties discussed the plan of action, finally deciding to mount an assault on the city of Damietta. King Louis was confident that he had learned enough from the past Crusader mistakes at the Egyptian city and hoped not to repeat them.

The Crusaders' stay at Cyprus was drawn out, however, as King Louis faced transportation problems, which halted his advance for seven months. This, paired with the lack of supplies, lowered the morale of the troops, with a good number of them deserting. Louis had to launch his offensive with less than half of the army he had started with. Even though the Crusaders had thought they would surprise the Egyptians with an attack on Damietta, the sultan had learned of the stationed Crusader army in Cyprus and had mobilized against them by sending reinforcements to the Egyptian heartland and evacuating the city. So, when King Louis and the

Crusaders landed on the beaches in June 1249, after being met with some resistance from the Egyptian forces, they were surprised to see Damietta undefended. They walked into the city and claimed it for themselves. After much consideration, a follow-up assault on Cairo was agreed upon.

However, just as in the case of the Fifth Crusade, the geographic challenges would prove to be a fatal enemy for the Christians, who got separated while trying to cross the Nile River in February 1250. The Egyptians, who had tried to avoid hand-to-hand combat as much as they could, saw an opening and quickly mobilized their troops. The part of the Christians that had crossed the river under Louis's brother, Richard of Artois, forced the Muslims to retreat to the town of Mansoura. Richard was adamant about chasing down the retreating forces, and he did not wait for the majority of the Crusader army to cross the river and be in range to support. This caused Richard's vanguard to be lured into more heavily fortified Egyptian positions. The Muslims were more aware of the geography of the region and outmaneuvered the Christians, leading them into a trap and massacring their front contingent. Nearly three hundred Templars lost their lives in the ensuing encounter, which was a heavy loss considering how much the members of the order contributed to the overall strength of the army. Guillaume de Sonnac was also wounded, losing an eye.

Three days later, when the rest of the Crusader force was in a position to attack, they managed to defeat whatever resistance the Muslims had put up outside the town of Mansoura. However, they were reluctant to continue with a siege, having suffered lots of casualties, including Grand Master Guillaume, who died on February 11th, 1250. This caused a lot of chaos and uncertainty in the ranks of the French. King Louis could not decide what to do and chose to wait outside the city, a decision that proved to be another mistake. The Egyptians quickly cut off the Crusaders' supply lines and made them heavily suffer from attrition and disease. In early April, Louis finally gave up and ordered a retreat. The Egyptians chased the Crusaders down, massacring nearly the whole army and capturing King Louis. The Seventh Crusade was yet another failure.

King Louis would eventually be released in exchange for the city of Damietta. The Crusaders, however, lacked the funds for the ransom of their king and asked the Templars for a massive sum of thirty thousand French livres, a demand that was first refused by the order on the grounds that Louis had not deposited money in the Temple, making the loan impossible. In the end, however, the Templars, under Marshal Reginald de Vichiers, were convinced to provide the necessary amount, realizing the urgency of the situation and making an exception for the king. King Louis, after his release, would form a good relationship with the Templars. He stayed in the Holy Land until 1254 and helped reunite the squabbling barons of the Latin kingdoms. With his endorsement, Reginald was elected as the new Grand Master of the Templars, and the king vowed to repay his debts to the order. In fact, Louis did much more for the development of Outremer than many previous kings had done in the past. He invested a lot of money into building up the defenses at towns like Jaffa and Acre and led the Holy Land into a relative period of stability, which was helped by the ten-year truce agreed with the Egyptians upon his release.

However, when King Louis departed, the Holy Land would once again descend into an unstable period, one characterized by war and internal power struggles. This time, the problem lay in the newly emerging threats both from the south in the form of the Mamluks gaining power in Egypt over the Ayyubid dynasty and in the northeast, as Outremer was about to be overrun by the Mongols.

The Christians of the East were very much aware of the Mamluks' capabilities; they had been elite slave warriors who had fought in the ranks of the Egyptians since the reign of Saladin. Over time, however, they had accumulated enough power to rise up and trample the dynasty, becoming the rulers of Egypt and posing a direct threat to the Holy Land. Their military supremacy would once again be proven when, in 1260, the Mamluks crushed the Mongol forces that had arrived at their doorstep near Nazareth. For some, this was a surprising development, as their two major enemies were fighting each other. However, the Templars had long been aware of the Mongols' activity and had correctly observed that they were fighting everyone they encountered on their way to the West, despite their religion or culture. In the late 1250s, some Templars in the region had urged for a build-up of fortifications of some of the cities, like Jaffa, and to abandon those sites that could not withhold a Mongol invasion. The order had also sent multiple envoys to Europe, describing the doom that was about to descend on the Holy Land in the form of the Mongol invasion.

With the victory against the Mongols and the accession to the throne of the Mamluk leader Baybars, Outremer was bound to be a target for the new sultan, who believed that the Christians had no right to exist in the East. He had also shown the Mongols how capable the Mamluk army was, forcing them to watch from the sidelines as he went on a campaign to rampage through the Christian lands. In the 1260s, Baybars ran over the Latin kingdoms, capturing one town after the other. The Christian military orders, which had bonded together despite their differences in internal political struggles, were unable to mount a significant resistance to the Mamluk advance. Arsuf, one of the most heavily fortified Hospitaller holdings, fell to the Egyptians, which was soon followed by the Templar castle of Safed.

The Templars tried to spend more and more resources in the desperate defense of their holdings, using their connections with King Louis to receive generous aid from France. However, it was not enough. Before the arrival of England's Prince Edward in 1272, the Latin kingdoms were almost completely conquered by their enemies. After Arsuf and Safed, the Mamluks had taken nearly all the coastal cities of the Holy Land, including Jaffa and Caesarea, as well as major fortifications in the region, like the Templar Castle of Beaufort and the Hospitaller Krak des Chevaliers. The situation looked dire, especially after the fall of Antioch in 1268 and the evacuation of the Templar castles in the Amanus March, a location the order had possessed since the very beginning of its days.

Thus, the arrival of Prince Edward, who had heard of the atrocities of the Mamluks and the Mongols from a Templar messenger in London and came to the Holy Land with reinforcements, gave some hope to the Christians of the Holy Land. However, the Englishman did not manage to improve the positions of the Latin kingdoms. He negotiated a ten-year truce with the Mamluks, as he had to return to London to be crowned as king in the wake of the passing of his father, Henry III.

Edward brought the news of the desperation of the Holy Land to Europe. The continent was shocked, and the talks for a new Crusade started. The new Templar Grand Master, William of Beaujeu, had realized that the future of the region was not looking too good, prompting him to go on a tour of Europe to gather whatever support he could for Outremer. In 1273, in a journey reminiscent of that of Hugues de Payens a century and a half prior, Grand Master William visited all the major European rulers to convince them to join a new Crusade. In 1274, a council assembled in Lyon to discuss the matter; however, in the end, no one decided to take up the cross, and William returned to Outremer empty-handed.

The following years saw heavy Templar involvement in the internal matters of the ongoing succession disputes in Tripoli and Jerusalem, with King Hugh of Cyprus being crowned the king of Jerusalem in 1269. He did not care to rule his kingdom from the Holy City and was instead isolated on his island. From there, Hugh observed as the rest of the Latin kingdoms were caught up in a civil war, blaming the order for being ignorant of what was good for the Christians. His distrust toward the Templars culminated in his assault on the Templar castle of Gastria on the island of Cyprus. As for the order, Grand Master William was trying to hold things together, but his involvement in the disputes of Tripoli was of no use. He managed to negotiate another truce with the Mamluks in 1282, but the peace was broken by the Egyptians, who had no more intention of dealing with the Christians.

The new Mamluk Sultan Qalawun embarked upon his quest of driving the Christians out of the Holy Land once and for all as soon as he ascended the throne of Egypt in mid-1285. The sultan stormed the Latin lands one by one, taking the port of Latakia and capturing the Hospitaller castle at al-Marqab by 1287. Learning of the sultan's intentions from an agent, Templar Grand Master William warned Tripoli twice about a potential invasion of the city, but the Tripolitans refused to listen. They had grown increasingly weary of the Grand Master after his involvement during the civil war, which lasted from 1277 to 1282. Consequently, Tripoli fell to Qalawun in the spring of 1289. Then, the Grand Master got intel about the next target of the Mamluks, the city of Acre, which was arguably the most heavily defended Christian holding of the East. But it was bound to fall without support, which was nowhere to be seen. William advised the people to evacuate the city or offer Qalawun something else, like a generous payment, in return, but he was once again The route of the Third Crusade.

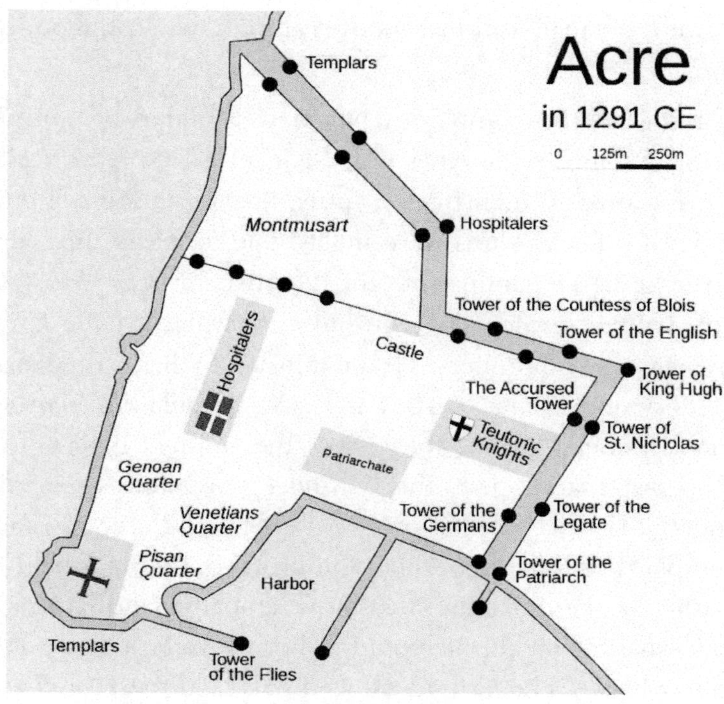

Acre in 1291

IYY, CC BY-SA 4.0 https://creativecommons.org/licenses/by-sa/4.0 via Wikimedia Commons https://commons.wikimedia.org/w/index.php?curid=92188862

Although Qalawun died in the early stages of the siege, his son, al-Ashraf Khalil, pledged to take the city and kill every Christian in it for his dying father, and the Mamluks rallied behind their new sultan. The Muslims started a long siege, building siege equipment for the assault and receiving reinforcements every day. With their backs against the wall, the Christians tried to negotiate, but their envoy was executed by the sultan. Even though Acre was heavily defended and well-supplied because the Christians still controlled the sea and were able to supply provisions, it was clear that they simply did not have enough men to repel an all-out Muslim attack.

Grand Master William realized this and decided to sally out of the city with a small but elite force to try and catch the besiegers off-guard and inflict at least some casualties. It was all in vain, however, as the Templars and the Hospitallers had to retreat because their horses were entangled in the enemy camp. They lost about twenty knights.

By mid-May, the bombardment was well underway, and its toll was being felt inside the city's walls. King Henry had arrived with about two thousand men from Cyprus, but it was still not enough. On May 18th, the Muslims were finally able to break through after three days of fierce fighting with the Templars and the Hospitallers at Saint Andrew's gate. The Muslims overwhelmed the Christian defenses by sheer numbers. Grand Master William died fighting. King Henry and a large part of the city's population managed to evacuate on ships, leaving the rest of the soldiers behind to fight until the last man. Soon, the Muslims were able to break the defenders at the city's center and were met with fierce resistance at the Templar headquarters, where the brothers put up a final stand. Eventually, the Templar commander, Theobald Gaudin, decided to flee with whatever wealth he could gather from the temple at Acre. The city was lost. The Crusaders, who had held the Holy Land for nearly two hundred years, were finally defeated.[16]

---

[16] Powell, J. M. (2007). "Church and Crusade: Frederick II and Louis IX." *The Catholic Historical Review*, 93(2), vi-264.

Martin, S. (2011). *The Knights Templar.* Oldcastle Books. Chapter 2.

Hill, P. (2018). *The Knights Templar at War, 1120-1312.* Pen & Sword Military. Part 2.

Welsh, W. E. (2016). "Crusader Catastrophe: The Battle of La Forbie." *Medieval Warfare*, 6(5), 26-33.

Jackson, P. (1987). "The Crusades of 1239-41 and Their Aftermath." *Bulletin of the School of Oriental and African Studies*, University of London, 50 (1), 32-60.

Chapter 10 – The Trial of the Knights Templar

After decades of fighting for the good of the Christians in the Holy Land, the Templars and, for that matter, the rest of the Latin kingdoms were finally defeated once and for all at Acre in 1291. The future, for the first time, seemed uncertain for the Knights Templar. Even though the order still held a lot of possessions and power in Europe, Outremer had always been their main base of operations, as well as their birthplace. While the Templars wanted to continue their existence in the West, the kings of Europe had other plans in mind. This chapter will look at the fate of the Knights Templar after the fall of Acre, diving deep into the final years of the order's existence in Europe, where a change of heart would prove to be fatal for the Templars.

After Acre

Theobald Gaudin fled to Sidon, taking with him what Templar wealth he could gather from the compound at Acre. There, he was elected as the new Grand Master, and the Templars tried to devise a plan of action against the Mamluks. However, they had no time. The invaders did not stop their offensive at Acre. After taking the city, they continued their advance on whatever Christian positions remained, capturing one Templar castle after another. The Muslims swept the remainder of the Holy Land throughout the summer of 1291, and Grand Master Theobald and the rest of the brothers were forced to flee to Cyprus, the only place in the East that remained somewhat out of reach from their enemies. By autumn, all of the famous Templar holdings were abandoned, with the brothers taking whatever they could with them and destroying whatever they could not. The Mamluks swiftly entered Sidon, then Haifa, and then took the castles of Tortosa and Atlit—a task no other invader had been able to successfully accomplish. By the end of 1291, the Templars were effectively out of Outremer. They would never again step foot in the Holy Land.

Limassol, a Templar fortress in Cyprus, was chosen as the new headquarters for the order, and the following year, Jacques de Molay succeeded Theobald as the new Grand Master. Jacques had spent about thirty years as a member of the order, and he would spend his time as the Grand Master wholeheartedly trying to restore the position of the Knights Templar in Outremer.

Grand Master Jacques de Molay
https://commons.wikimedia.org/w/index.php?curid=2612812

Unlike some of the previous leaders of the order, who were more concerned with gaining power for themselves by getting involved in the complex politics and acting from behind the scenes, Grand Master Jacques had much clearer motivations. In addition to Cyprus, the order held the small island of Ruad just off the coast of Palestine, which the Grand Master thought to be a valuable resource in conducting new operations in Outremer. He did not want to give up on the dream of the Christians returning to the Holy Land, but he was disappointed when he was informed of the island's loss to the Mamluks, who had realized the importance of the Templar holding there and stormed it in 1302. In a way, this was the final blow to any hope of regaining the lost territories. Jacques de Molay had tried getting help from the West in the mid-

1290s during his visit to Europe, but he had been unsuccessful. No major European power wanted to contribute to the restoration of the Holy Land, as they were well aware of the costs of a potential expedition.

On the surface, however, Europe was still sympathetic to the Templar Order. In 1294, during his visit, Jacques de Molay had spoken to Pope Boniface VIII, and his holiness granted him and the rest of the Templars the same privileges they had held in Jerusalem. Essentially, the pope tried to make it clear that the order was still respected, despite the loss of the Holy Land. Some subtle help also came from different European kings, who offered benefits like exemption from certain taxes to help the struggling Templars. Unfortunately for Jacques de Molay, the biggest supporter of the Templars, Edward I of England, was occupied on two fronts, as he was fighting with France and Scotland at the time and could not offer reinforcements to the Grand Master, although he did promise similar economic benefits. All in all, it seemed clear that the *Reconquista* of the Holy Land or another Crusade was only possible in the distant future—a future the Templars would not be able to see.

The Templars were not the only ones unsure of their future. The other two military orders, the Hospitallers and the Teutons, were also forced to abandon their possessions in the Holy Land and escape to the West. It seemed that all three orders had lost their original purpose since there were no more Christians in the East for them to defend. They all adapted to the situation differently. The Hospitallers, for example, adopted the previously overlooked responsibility of patrolling the seas and played an important role in the maritime matters of the Mediterranean. At first, they followed the Templars and dwelled in Cyprus, but they quickly made the island of Rhodes their main base of operations and slowly started building up their resources both on the sea and on land. As for the Teutons, they relocated north to the port city of Marienburg in

Prussia. From there, they spent centuries fighting against the pagans in eastern Europe, becoming increasingly involved in the politics of the region. They eventually established their own sovereign state. Thus, the three military orders continued their existence.

Philip against the Templars

Due to the shadow that was cast over the future of the military orders right after the fall of Acre, there were talks of a potential merge of the Knights Templar and Knights Hospitaller. The argument for the unification of the two institutions was mainly the fact that they would be more competent at conducting their future affairs since both orders had been significantly weakened by the loss of the Holy Land. The Teutons were not a part of this conversation, perhaps because of the way they had always distinguished themselves from the Hospitallers and Templars due to their Germanic origin. However, immediately after the fall of Acre, no one really had time to consider a unification of the orders, and, thus, the matter was mostly ignored by all parties.

In 1305, the talks would commence once again of a potential merge of the Templars and the Hospitallers. This time, Pope Clement V was the initiator. The pope invited Jacques de Molay and his Hospitaller counterpart, Foulques de Villaret, to discuss the issue. Jacques de Molay was still not sold on the idea, claiming that the two orders were separate entities, and although their functions often intertwined, they would better function if left separate. In fact, when he arrived in Paris in late 1306 to discuss the matter, he made a sound argument, but the pope was still not convinced. The two waited for Grand Master Foulques to arrive before decisively deciding anything. The Hospitaller had been delayed in Rhodes because of some domestic issues.

At that time, another matter popped up on the agenda. Pope Clement was curious about the allegations he had heard about the Templar Order. According to the rumors, behind the image of a virtuous Christian military order was actually a sinful institution that secretly conducted sinful and inappropriate practices. There were even allegations of heresy and sodomy. The Grand Master, of course, denied everything the pope said to him and told the pope that he would allow the papacy to investigate the order to clear up any doubts. In turn, the pope sent a letter to Philip IV of France, requesting the king to conduct a thorough inquiry. The anti-Templar sentiment had grown the strongest in France.

However, the matter was much more serious than either the pope or Jacques de Molay had thought. On Friday, October 13th, 1307, all the Templars in France were arrested, including their Grand Master. It was a move that shocked Christendom and forever changed the legacy of the Knights Templar.

But why exactly did King Philip IV of France, the ruler who would come to be known as Philip the Fair, arrest the Templars? At the time of the arrest, nobody was sure, and Europe did not know how to react. The order had been a well-respected organization that had always served the interests of Christians. Not only that, but they were under the direct protection of the pope. No monarch had the authority to prosecute the Templars without permission from the papacy. In any case, some thought that this unexpected move from Philip was unjustified. It is true that Philip was an extraordinarily pious ruler, but he was also arrogant and power-hungry. The Templars, at the time of his ascension to the throne, were one of the wealthiest actors in the whole of Europe. Thus, his motivations may have been to seize the valuable Templar possessions he knew existed in his country.

In fact, King Philip is known to have overexercised his power on a couple of occasions. For example, he had seized the assets of the French Jews just a year earlier in 1306 to gather more funds for the French economy, which had been deprived of income due to warring with England. Later on, he would do the same thing with the Italian bankers from Lombardy. In addition to all of this, in 1303, because of his "pious" nature, he tried to kidnap Pope

Boniface VIII and bring him to France to make the pope face virtually the same charges the Templars later faced. In any case, although the move was unexpected, Philip was prone to making extraordinary decisions. It appears that he had sent out the plan for the arrest of the Templars in September. Therefore, he must have been prepared for what was about to happen.

The main charges set against the Templars were heresy, blasphemy, and sodomy—a combination of words that had never been associated with the order. However, the Inquisition was already well underway, so Christians were aware of the consequences if one was to be found guilty of those charges. Europe was very fearful of the alleged witches who practiced magic and had witnessed the Inquisitors publicly burn and hang every heretic they could find. The accusations against the Templars were nothing new to the people, partially because Philip had used similar accusations against Pope Boniface. The public had a mixed reaction to the Templars' arrest. Pope Clement, for example, condemned Philip's actions in a letter he sent to the king on October 25th, saying that the Templars were under the protection of the papacy and that he had no right to arrest them without proof.

However, by the time the pope wrote the letter, the Templars had already been put on trial at the University of Paris. At the assembly, the arrested Templars, including Jacques de Molay, confessed to the crimes they had committed. The Grand Master confessed to denying Christ and spitting on the cross, shocking the assembly and starting a public upheaval in Paris. The people took to the streets and demanded the execution of the Templars. Pope Clement, who was now pressured to act because the Templars had admitted their guilt, signed a bull a month later, ordering the arrest of all brothers throughout Europe. This, in turn, prompted different reactions in different kingdoms. For instance, England, Portugal, and Aragon were reluctant to prosecute the Templars because of the close ties the rulers held with the order. The whole of the

Catholic world was in disbelief but complied with the pope's orders. In the following months, most of the Templars were sent to prisons.

Depiction of Baphomet
https://commons.wikimedia.org/w/index.php?curid=45656

In the prisons, the brothers would be forced to confess their sins, often through torture. By then, the Inquisition was involved, and despite it being a structure under the papacy, it very much served the interests of the French king. Thus, the Templars were tortured, and not a lot of them could endure it. In the end, when they finally broke, they spoke of unheard atrocities they had practiced in secret in different Templar compounds around the world. Many brothers admitted to taking part in the violation of the cross by spitting and urinating on it, followed by denying Christ as the Messiah; they recognized him as nothing more than a prophet. Templars also spoke of acts of sodomy, which took place during their reception ceremonies and included requiring the brothers to kiss each other on erotic parts of the body in order to be fully accepted into the order. Some also spoke of breaking celibacy and having indulged in sex with women. Perhaps the most heretical act confessed by a number of Templar brothers was praying to a demonic deity called Baphomet. This creature's description varied according to different Templars but is largely depicted as a goat-headed man with wings and has become associated with satanic rituals.

The Trials

Months after the start of the Templars' imprisonment, Pope Clement finally requested the Templars to be heard in front of him and a papal committee. On December 24th, 1307, the court was convened, and Jacques de Molay and several high-ranking Templars were brought forth to discuss their charges. However, unlike before, Grand Master Jacques and the rest of the brothers retracted their confessions, claiming that they had only confessed to the Inquisition to escape torture. This was a crucial development, and it confused the assembled audience, including King Philip and his righthand man Guillaume de Nogaret, a man with just as fanatical views as the French king. By retracting their confessions, the Templars stalled the hearings, forcing the pope to suspend the proceedings for the foreseeable future until further proof could be collected.

Philip was furious. He had hoped for the order's quick capitulation, as he could then seize the wealth of the Templars for himself and solve his financial troubles. After the suspension of the hearings, he was desperate to regain public support. He even assembled the Estates General for the first time in history to see how the people felt about the trials, but he was disappointed to see that the majority of the assembled population was still very sympathetic toward the Templars. By then, the king hardly tried to hide the fact that he was exerting influence over the papacy, forcing the pope and his lawyers to reside in Paris, where they worked meticulously on the matter. From time to time, Philip would send several Templars he knew had confessed to the pope, but the official hearings would not continue until November of 1309.

The renewal of the official papal hearings on November 26th saw Grand Master Jacques de Molay speak once again to the assembly. This time, however, it was completely different than what he had said a year earlier. The Templar Grand Master publicly expressed that he was unfit to defend the order against the charges, saying that he had no legal training or counseling. Philip saw this as a victory and made sure to spread the word that the Grand Master had refused to defend his brethren, going as far as to shame him in front of the imprisoned Templars.

The following February, however, two Templar brothers by the names of Reginald of Provins and Peter de Bologna stepped up to defend the order; they were the only ones with a legal background among the brothers. In April, after yet another renewal of the hearings, the two Templars made quite a case of the order's innocence. They told the court that the allegations against them were all made-up. It was just a part of Philip's cunning scheme to undermine the Templars' power and gain their wealth for himself. In addition, they spoke of the torture they had to endure, claiming that the Inquisitors would only be done once they heard what they wanted to hear.

This caused outrage in France. After the end of the hearings, Philip realized he was in a desperate situation. His plan had failed, and he needed an alternative, which for him, being the arrogant king that he was, was a more tyrannical approach. Philip received more legal counseling and carefully weighed the stakes. On May 11th, 1310, he declared that all Templars who had retracted their confessions were to be found guilty, accusing them of being relapsed heretics. The following day, fifty-four Templars were sentenced to death. Since they were considered heretics, they received the most painful and dreadful punishment: death by fire. Still, this was not the end since the hearings were still planned to continue.

The following year, in 1311, the Council of Vienne convened. The Templar matter would finally be decided once and for all. It is important to mention that the pope and the assembled clergy were under immense pressure from King Philip, with the French king sending a small armed contingent to "oversee" and "protect" the pope in case anything went wrong. Seven Templars were brought forth and given a chance to speak and defend their order. However, it was all in vain.

Despite the pressure the pope faced from the king, his next decisions did not fully please Philip. On October 20th, 1311, he signed a new bull titled *Vox in excelso* and formally dissolved the order. However, according to the pope, the Templars were not found guilty of the charges set against them. Clement would issue another bull in the following spring, *Ad providam*, where he declared that all Templar possessions should be given to the Knights Hospitaller, shattering Philip's hopes of seizing the fortune for himself. Finally, the third papal bull, *Considerantes dudum*, allowed separate provinces to prosecute the Templars separately, restating that the charges were not to be discussed as a whole but instead according to whichever Templars had been captured. By doing this, the prosecution of the Templars was a papal matter, and the Inquisition was to handle the rest of it. Little did he know that the Inquisition, despite being a papal institution, had become increasingly independent and had developed similar fanatical Christian views as King Philip and his henchmen.

There was still the question of what should be done with Jacques de Molay and the three other high-ranking Templars who had been imprisoned with him. In December 1313, the question was finally addressed when Clement and the clergy started yet another series of meetings. It had been almost seven years since the Grand Master had been captured at the Paris Temple. By March 1314, time had certainly taken its toll on Jacques de Molay. The Grand Master, Geoffroi (Geoffrey) de Charney, Hugues de Pairaud, and Geoffroi de Gonneville were brought forward on a special platform at Notre Dame, where the inquisitors read out the council's decision. All four of them were sentenced to indefinite imprisonment. The Templars were publicly shamed once again for being heretics, only being saved from death by the grace of the pope.

Before they could be brought back to the cells, however, Jacques de Molay had a final thing to say. Without permission from the guards who accompanied him, he lashed out, shouting out a retraction of the confessions he had made earlier and speaking of the order's innocence. He adamantly defended his brethren, something he had failed to do for all these years. Motivated by the Grand Master, Geoffroi de Charney joined in and claimed that he was innocent, while the rest were swiftly taken back to their cells. Of course, the guards eventually reacted and seized both Jacques and Geoffroi. It was a desperate move, and arguably, both Templars knew that by publicly retracting their confessions, they were signing their own death warrants. King Philip was quick to act, as everyone had heard of the spectacle at Notre Dame. He assembled his council and declared the two Templars to be relapsed heretics.

At Ile aux Javiaux, in front of a crowd that had gathered to witness the final moments of the Templars, Grand Master Jacques de Molay and Preceptor of Normandy Geoffroi de Charney were publicly stripped of their clothes, tied to wooden stakes, and set ablaze. As the Templars burned, their whole order collapsed with them. Jacques de Molay wished both Pope Clement and King Philip to meet him before God within a year, while Geoffroi de Charney continued to shout of his innocence and loyalty to his Grand Master. The Knights Templar had fallen.[17]

---

[17] Martin, S. (2011). *The Knights Templar.* Oldcastle Books. Chapter 3.

Julien Théry. (2013). "A Heresy of State: Philip the Fair, the Trial of the 'Perfidious Templars,' and the Pontificalization of the French Monarchy." *Journal of Medieval Religious Cultures,* 39 (2), 117-148.

Chapter 11 – Templar Secrets and Legacy

Thus, after nearly two hundred years of existence, the Knights Templar was destroyed. Jacques de Molay was the last Grand Master, and the order would never see the light of day ever again. Most Templars in Europe were imprisoned, and over time, the image of the Knights Templar would transform into a myth. This chapter will briefly cover the twisted legacy of the Templar Order, taking a look at the rumors and secrets that have been associated with the order since the very beginning. We will also try to explain why the Templars became such a mythicized phenomenon.

After 1314

The Templar Order was officially disbanded, and its Grand Master was publicly executed by 1314. However, in some parts of

---

Perkins, C. (1909). "The Trial of the Knights Templars in England." *The English Historical Review*, 24 (95), 432–447.

Nicholson, H. J. (2011). *The Knights Templar on Trial: The Trial of the Templars in the British Isles, 1308–11.* History Press.

Field, S. L. (2016). "Torture and Confession in the Templar Interrogations at Caen, 28-29 October 1307." *Speculum*, 91 (2), 297–327.

the world, the brothers who still roamed free tried to overcome the challenges presented to them in different ways. Despite the formal dissolution of the order, King Philip was deprived of its wealth and numerous invaluable possessions. The king's agents were disappointed to find out that most of the Templar records, which were held in the Paris Temple, had disappeared, as had a lot of the wealth the king knew was located there.

La Rochelle

In fact, it is believed that somehow the Templars knew about their grim future before 1307, as most of the order's treasure seems to have been evacuated by the time the trials began. Before the arrests, most documents in the Templars' possession are believed to have been burned by Jacques de Molay, and the riches are thought to have been taken to the Templar holding of La Rochelle, which acted as the main naval base of operations for the order. Located on the coast of the Atlantic in southeastern France, Templar ships frequently sailed to La Rochelle; however, what they carried has never been identified. Even after the fall of the order, the castle contained nothing suspicious and certainly nothing valuable. Plus, there was no sign of the Templar navy.

As for the members of the order, they continued living in different parts of Europe. Most Templars may have been arrested and tortured throughout France, Germany, and parts of Italy, but Iberia and Britain still remained relatively friendly toward the brothers. In Portugal and Aragon, where the Templars were not found guilty after the trials, the Templars took a new name, Knights of Christ, and continued serving in a military role as they had before. In fact, over time, the Knights of Christ became increasingly involved in exploration, funding many expeditions to the New World. Famous explorers like Vasco da Gama and Christopher Columbus both had connections to this order (a fact that might explain the red cross on many of Columbus's ships that sailed to the Americas). Although the theory that says the Templars discovered the Americas is still seen as far-fetched and has never been proven, those Templars who did survive and transformed into the Knights of Christ continued to exist.

In other parts of the world, the Templars adapted to the situation differently. Some are thought to have joined the Hospitallers and the Teutons due to the closeness between these organizations. Not long after the fall of the Templar Order, the Templars are believed to have even fought in Scotland, as several sources tell of their involvement with the Scottish Robert the Bruce, which eventually led to the founding of the Scots Guards and, later on, the Freemasons.

Templar involvement has also been speculated in Switzerland, a state that quickly managed to become one of the strongest military powers in the 14th century, despite its small size. The Templars are thought to have bolstered the Swiss army, making it a small but elite and disciplined force. This theory is further supported by the idea of the Templars sharing their banking knowledge in Switzerland, laying the foundations for the famous Swiss banking traditions. All in all, those Templars who survived the purge did not just cease to exist. As the brothers had done countless times in the past, they adapted to the challenges they faced.

The Mysterious Knights of Solomon

In addition to their extraordinary two-hundred-year history, during which the Templars became the biggest military order and one of the most influential actors in Crusader world politics, the order has also risen to popularity because of the mysterious nature that surrounds it. In fact, many contemporary chroniclers and historical figures, as well as modern historians and scholars, firmly believe that even though King Philip's main motive was to seize the riches of the Templars for himself, there must have been some truth in the allegations made against the Knights Templar. Although not a lot of evidence of their heretical activities has been found, it is unwise to imagine that the suspicions were not based on anything.

Perhaps this sense of mystery about the order is caused by the lack of reliable written sources, which, in turn, technically makes everything we have mentioned up to this point questionable. Still, the Templars were mysterious in every aspect of their lives, with the subtle exception being their role in the politics of the time and their military actions. For instance, there is even a debate surrounding the origins of the order, as many believe that it originated much earlier than 1119. Different chronicles tell of different years and events at the beginning of the order's existence, making it unclear when exactly it was founded and how many members there were initially. In addition, the lack of official Templar documents before the Council of Troyes is highly suspicious due to the fact that the Templars were a Christian organization, making some believe that the order was, at first, a military institution and only became Christian after Hugues de Payens's visit to Europe. In any case, the actual dates and the conflicting details about the Templars' early days are the least mysterious thing about them.

There seem to be more intriguing details that have never really been explained. One of those is certainly the mystery surrounding the Temple Mount and the alleged excavations of the Templars at their headquarters. The Al-Aqsa Mosque has always been a subject of much speculation. Some believed that there was great treasure buried below the Templar headquarters and that they started out there because they knew of the treasure. In addition, by the time the king of Jerusalem gave them the Temple Mount, it was not in good shape and had been partially destroyed. Why would the Templars accept such a place? Did they want to spend years and countless resources rebuilding it? Some believe that they were looking for something, maybe an ancient Christian relic, some document about the origins of Christianity, or even the Ark of the Covenant. Maybe they found it; nobody knows for sure.

A stained-glass depiction of the Holy Grail

After all, various relics have been connected to the Templars. For example, the Holy Grail, the cup from which Jesus drank at the Last Supper, has come to be associated with the order. Some think it may have been because of Troyes, the city where the first fables about the magic nature of the grail were written and where the Templars got their start. Still, this connection has never been proven, and the myth of the Holy Grail pops up all throughout Europe with different explanations for its powers and origins.

As for the alleged Templar practices of heresy, there is still the question of what is logical to believe and what is not. Close Templar ties to Catharism, a Gnostic movement in southern France that originated in the 12th century, is seen as a reason to believe the order was open to heretical tendencies. The Cathars were recognized as a heretical sect and the enemies of the papacy, but the Templars openly accepted them in their ranks, especially at places like Languedoc, where the Cathars, according to some accounts, even outnumbered the brothers. Grand Master Bertrand de Blanchefort also came from a Cathar background, making it feasible that there was a much deeper connection between the sect and the order. The Templars have also been linked with other less prominent heresies, like the Johannites and the Cult of Mary Magdalene and the Virgin Mary, underlining their potential keenness for John the Baptist. The members of the Johannites saw him as the real messiah, and the two women were also thought to have been the faces of God, making its members goddess-worshipers.

Most often, however, the Templar connections with the Muslim world have been underlined as a reason to believe that the members of the order had diverged from Christianity. The brothers were suspiciously close to the Muslims. After all, the Templars often made alliances with different Muslim rulers to strengthen their own power in the region. Still, over time, they became more and more open toward the Muslims and did not outright see them as enemies as they had in the beginning. They exchanged knowledge and became more and more aware of Muslim traditions and their lifestyle, sometimes even adopting parts of it. For this reason, the Christians confronted the brothers countless times, believing that they had developed a much deeper, intimate relationship with the Muslim world than was acceptable.

Some say the order was conducting secret satanic rituals, including worshiping demonic deities, in their holdings. This is probably the most trumped-up charge set against the Templars by King Philip. We have mentioned Baphomet, a mysterious creature that was associated with a satanic cult. What has been speculated is that, despite its various descriptions by different captured Templars, Baphomet may have just been a life-sized head with magical powers to make the lands fertile. The Templars are known to have kept heads in their compounds, like that of Saint Euphemia of Chalcedon, which was preserved in Cyprus. This "obsession" with heads may have originated from the Muslim world, namely the Assassins, who are known to have buried the new members of their organization up to their heads as part of their reception ceremony. On the other hand, Baphomet may have just been a translation error from the word Mahomet—the French for Prophet Muhammad. Still, whether or not the Templars actually worshiped Baphomet in the first place has not been proven, and stretching this theory to assume that Baphomet was actually Muhammad is even more unwise if we want to maintain historical objectivity.

Out of all the charges set against the Templars, the one with the most backing was denying Christ—a practice that was remarked in the Chinon Parchment, a papal document from 1308 that describes some of the confessions of the imprisoned Templars. According to the document, the Templars admitted that spitting, urinating and spitting on the cross, and denouncing Christ was part of the reception ceremony for a new member, but it was only done to imitate the torture the brothers would have to endure if they ever fell in the hands of the Muslims. Whether or not this is true, it was certainly not a good look for the order and gave rise to further suspicions about its mysterious nature.

Conclusion

Overall, the Knights Templar found its own unique place in history. Over the course of its short existence, the order managed to become much more than a group of Christian knights devoted to the noble cause of protecting traveling pilgrims. The ongoing processes reshaped the order's purpose so much that, at first glance, one can be astonished at why the Templars diverged from the simple path that had been chosen by Hugues de Payens. While this remark is logical, we should not forget that the Templars existed in a complex political landscape and had to adapt to the ever-changing power struggles of the Christian and Muslim worlds. The truth of the matter is that the privileges granted to the order signify its distinct, almost invaluable nature and, if nothing else, shows that the Templars deserved whatever praise and love they received in their lifetime.

As for the secrets surrounding the order, the Knights Templar just cannot be separated from its mystery, despite the efforts of numerous historians and scholars. In fact, it is the mythical nature of the Templars that makes them so interesting. We do not really know if the members of the order were just ordinary men or part of a larger secret society that continued to exist even after 1314. The various myths and theories about the darker side of the Templars define their uniqueness and provide an intriguing point of view to look at and analyze the order.

All in all, throughout the course of this book, we have observed the two-hundred-year history of the Knights Templar and analyzed how the order transformed during this period in response to the events that happened. From just nine knights to a global superpower, it is safe to say that the Templars were successfully able to overcome the challenges they were presented with until they were dissolved.

The brothers were pioneers in many aspects of life. They were not only spectacular warriors but also exemplary Christians, inventing a completely new standard for medieval knights. Their contributions to socio-economic life should also not be forgotten, as the Templars were way ahead of their time, essentially becoming the first bankers of Europe. For these reasons, we may never see an organization quite like the Knights Templar again.

Here's another book by Enthralling History that you might like

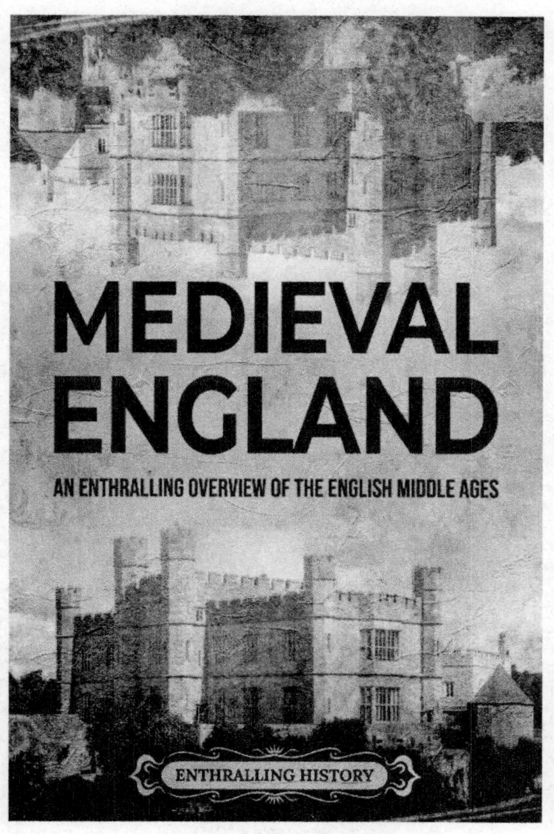

Free limited time bonus

Stop for a moment. We have a free bonus set up for you. The problem is this: we forget 90% of everything that we read after 7 days. Crazy fact, right? Here's the solution: we've created a printable, 1-page pdf summary for this book that you're reading now. All you have to do to get your free pdf summary is to go to the following website: **https://livetolearn.lpages.co/enthrallinghistory/**

Once you do, it will be intuitive. Enjoy, and thank you!

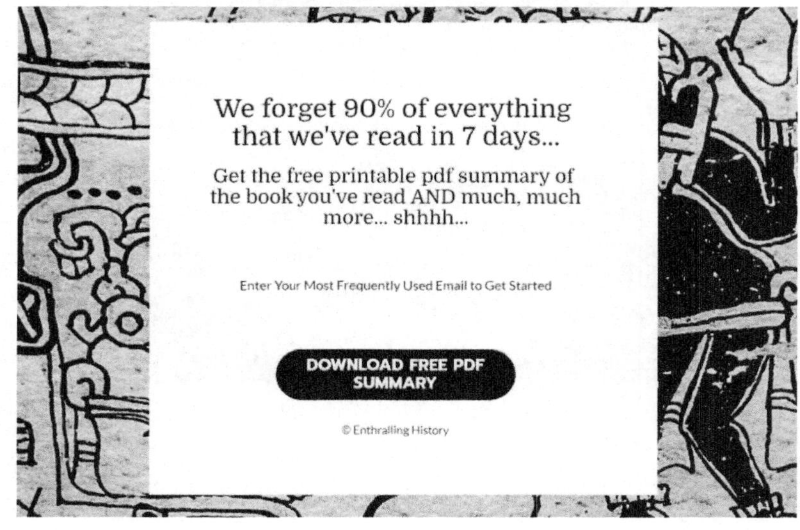

References:

Barber, M. C. (1984). "The Social Context of the Templars." *Transactions of the Royal Historical Society, 34,* 27–46. https://doi.org/10.2307/3679124

Blanchet, M. (2021). "Chapter 5: The Patriarchs and the Union of the Churches." In *A Companion to the Patriarchate of Constantinople.* Leiden, The Netherlands: Brill. doi: https://doi.org/10.1163/9789004424470_006.

Brand, C. M. (1962). "The Byzantines and Saladin, 1185-1192: Opponents of the Third Crusade." *Speculum, 37*(2), 167–181. https://doi.org/10.2307/2849946.

Coureas, N. (2013). "The Conquest of Cyprus during the Third Crusade According to Greek Chronicles from Cyprus." *The Medieval Chronicle, 8,* 193–204. https://www.jstor.org/stable/48577683.

Faith, J. (2011). *The Knights Templar in Somerset.* History Press.

Ferris, E. (1902). "The Financial Relations of the Knights Templars to the English Crown." *The American Historical Review, 8*(1), 1-17. https://doi.org/10.2307/1832571.

Field, S. L. (2016). "Torture and Confession in the Templar Interrogations at Caen, 28-29 October 1307." *Speculum, 91*(2), 297–327. http://www.jstor.org/stable/43883958.

Forey, A. (2004). "The Siege of Lisbon and the Second Crusade. Portuguese Studies, 20, 1–13." http://www.jstor.org/stable/41105214.
Frankopan, P. (2012). *The First Crusade: The Call from the East.* Belknap Press of Harvard University Press. Retrieved January 31, 2022.
Gilmour-Bryson, A. (1996). "Sodomy and the Knights Templar." *Journal of the History of Sexuality, 7*(2), 151–183. http://www.jstor.org/stable/3704138.
Hill, P. (2018). *The Knights Templar at War, 1120–1312.* Pen & Sword Military.
Humphreys, R. S. (1977). *From Saladin to the Mongols: The Ayyubids of Damascus, 1193-1260.* SUNY Press.
Julien Théry. (2013). "A Heresy of State: Philip the Fair, the Trial of the 'Perfidious Templars,' and the Pontificalization of the French Monarchy." *Journal of Medieval Religious Cultures, 39*(2), 117–148. https://doi.org/10.5325/jmedirelicult.39.2.0117.
Lotan, S. (2015). "The Teutonic Knights and their Attitude about Muslims: Saracens in the Latin Kingdom of Jerusalem and in the Baltic Region." *Fear and Loathing in the North: Jews and Muslims in Medieval Scandinavia and the Baltic Region,* 313-328.
Lourie, E. (1975). "The Will of Alfonso I, 'El Batallador,' King of Aragon and Navarre: A Reassessment." *Speculum,* 50 (4), 635–651. https://doi.org/10.2307/2855471.
Martin, S. (2011). *The Knights Templar.* Oldcastle Books.
Murphy, P. (2012). "The Vatican Secret Archive: A History." *Seanchas Ardmhacha: Journal of the Armagh Diocesan Historical Society,* 24 (1), 240–249. http://www.jstor.org/stable/43869514
Napier, G. (2011). *The Rise and Fall of the Knights Templar.* History Press.
Nicholson, H. J. (2011). *The Knights Templar on Trial: The Trial of the Templars in the British Isles, 1308–11.* History Press.
Nowell, C. E. (1947). "The Old Man of the Mountain." *Speculum, 22*(4), 497–519. https://doi.org/10.2307/2853134

Perkins, C. (1909). "The Trial of the Knights Templars in England." *The English Historical Review*, 24 (95), 432–447. http://www.jstor.org/stable/550361

Powell, J. M. (2007). "Church and Crusade: Frederick II and Louis IX." *The Catholic Historical Review*, 93 (2), vi–264. http://www.jstor.org/stable/25166835.

Somerville, R. (1974). The Council of Clermont (1095), and Latin Christian Society." *Archivum Historiae Pontificiae*, 12, 55–90. http://www.jstor.org/stable/23563638.

Valente, J. (1998). "The New Frontier: The Role of the Knights Templar in the Establishment of Portugal as an Independent Kingdom." *Mediterranean Studies, 7*, 49–65. http://www.jstor.org/stable/41166860.

Welsh, W. E. (2016). "Crusader Catastrophe: The Battle of La Forbie." *Medieval Warfare, 6*(5), 26–33. https://www.jstor.org/stable/48578609

Willoughby, J. (2012). "A Templar Chronicle of the Third Crusade: Origin and Transmission." *Medium Ævum, 81*(1), 126–134. https://doi.org/10.2307/43632903

Napier, G. (2011). The Rise and Fall of the Knights Templar. History Press. Chapter 4.

Gilmour-Bryson, A. (1996). "Sodomy and the Knights Templar." Journal of the History of Sexuality, 7 (2), 151–183.

Murphy, P. (2012). "The Vatican Secret Archive: A History." Seanchas Ardmhacha: Journal of the Armagh Diocesan Historical Society, 24 (1), 240–249.

Printed in Great Britain
by Amazon

46057308R00106